Warren's Look Back

Warren Lupel

Disclaimer

ANDREW CALCUTT

Dear Warren,

Thank you very much for taking the time to meet with mu couple weeks ago. Congratulations on your mat move and semi-retirement.

I really enjoyed discussing the practice with you and it's easy to see why Karen calls you a great mentor. I really appreciated your thoughts on work and ideas for ways to become a litigator for. Thank you again. Jery, truly yours.

Andrew

April 27,1999

Dear Sonny,

Words could never express my gratitude to you. It was you and your skills – well known to the ARDC that, I am sure, tilted the scales for me.

You helped get me through the toughest 14 Mos. of my life. I found that your lawyering got me focused on my career.

With the utmost of thanks.

H

ANDREW CALCUTT

Dear Warren,

Thank you very much for taking the time to meet with me a couple weeks ago. Congratulations on your next move and semi-retirement.

I really enjoyed discussing the practice with you and it's easy to see why Karen calls you a great mentor. I really appreciated your thoughts on potential work and ideas for ways to become a better litigator. Thank you again. Very Truly Yours,
Andrew

April 27, 1999

Dear Sonny,

Words could never express my gratitude to you. It was you and your skills — well known to the ARK. that, I am sure, tilted the scales for me.

You helped get me through the toughest 14 mos. of my life. I found that your lawyering got me focused on my career. with the utmost of thanks
#

4

Dear Mr. Warren Lupel:

I want to take this opportunity to "THANK you", From the bottom of my heart, For All that you HAVE DONE FOR ME. Your kindness Anal sincerity is greatly appreciated. May your Holidays be filled with Joy. THANK you!!

- Ennedy D. Riwere

Dear Mr. Warren Lupel:

I want to take this opportunity to "THANK YOU", from the bottom of my heart, for all that you have done for me. Your kindness and sincerity is greatly appreciated. May your Holidays be filled with Joy. THANK YOU!!

— Ennedy D. Rivera

Check for #615

3-6-09

Dear Warren,

I sat down the other day with a yellow pad to make some notes that I wanted to send to you with my thoughts about my JIB experience After about 2 pages, the thought finally struck me that this case is over & it's time to move on!

So... I won't go into all of that. Instead, let me just say Thank-you! Your closing argument was exceptional-clear, concise & it conveyed so much of what I wanted to communicate to the Board. Most importantly, the case is finished & I have been permitted to proceed with my judicial career.

Thank you again! with warmest personal regards,

Tom Little.

3-6-09

Dear Warren,

I sat down the other day with a yellow pad to make some notes that I wanted to send to you with my thoughts about my JIB experience. After about 2 pages, the thought finally struck me that this case is over + it's time to move on!

So... I won't go into all of that. Instead, let me just say Thank-you! Your closing argument was exceptional - clear, concise + it conveyed so much of what I wanted to communicate to the Board. Most importantly, the case is finished + I have been permitted to proceed with my judicial career.

Thank you again! With warmest personal regards,
Tom Little.

check for #615

8

Warren,

In a lifetime, some are fortunate to know people that are truly a blessing -

That would be you.

You have a wonderful way

of going out of your way

to be wonderful.

Thank you so much!

Happy New Year!

Binda Brooks

Warren,

In a lifetime, some are fortunate to know people that are truly a blessing —

That would be you.

You have a wonderful way

of going out of your way

to be wonderful.

Thank you so much!

Happy New Year!
Linda Brooks

Warren,

My wife and I cannot put into words our thanks.to you. I am eternally indebted to you for the literally breathtaking (I MEAN IT) defense of case Not only did you leave no stone unturned, you pummeled into dust every stone they were hurling at me. While doing that you at all times were a gentle man your style- the deep voice and the polished Vocabulary made you a tremendous advocate for your clients. You ruled moral authority which was forcefully wert at the trial. May you be blessed by God with health, Prosperity and Mazel. Thank you peter.

Warren,

My wife and I cannot put into words our thanks to you. I am eternally indebted to you for the literally breathtaking (I MEAN IT) defense of my case. Not only did you leave no stone unturned, you pummelled into dust every stone they were hurling at me. While doing that you at all times were a gentleman. Your style — the deep voice and the polished vocabulary make you a tremendous advocate for your clients. You exuded moral authority which was forcefully used at the trial. May you be blessed by G-d with health, prosperity and Mazel. Thank you — Peter

"WAHOO!
YOU RULE!
WOO! WOO! WOO!"

-Me

WARREN,

With the game tied you hit a home run out of the park with bases loaded. You are a fantastic terrific lawyer and a polished gentleman. My wife and I are eternally indebted to you.

Peter & Coura Whethrop

"WAHOO!
YOU RULE!
WOO! WOO! WOO!"

—ME

WARREN,

WITH THE GAME TIED YOU HIT A HOME RUN OUT OF THE PARK WITH BASES LOADED. YOU ARE A FANTASTIC TERRIFIC LAWYER AND A POLISHED GENTLEMAN. MY WIFE and I are eternally indebted to you.

Peter + Laura Whittrop

Dear Warren,

Following the trial, I stopped at the leather school in Florence to get this for you. Truly I appreciate your expertise, professionalism and skill.

Thank you

11-10-01

Dear Warren,

Following the trial, I stopped at the leather school in Florence to get this for you. Truly, I appreciate your expertise, professionalism, and skill. Thank you

Maureen Julia Taylor

Mr & Mrs Hupel

I always want to express my gratitude for the help you've given me Though due relied less on you to answer specific questions in the recent past, I have still relied on the thoughtful decision making processer I have developed. This development is in large part due to you mr Hupel. I am grateful to both of you for always making me comfortable in your home and also bring thoughtful, dignified people whom I view as mates for myself. Thank you both and I'll talk to you soon

Sincerely

Thank you
for adding such a happy note
to the holidays!
THANKS AGAIN
AND A HAPPY NEW YEAR

Dear Warren,

I first want to pay and convey my thanks to you for all you have done for us.

It took about a year for the good news to come in! We were trying very hard to prepare for the worst. It was difficult to accept the best.

Thanks to you we can now resume our lives in a normal frame time (efforts are being done low to do that!).

Thank you from the bottom of my heart. Sincerely,

Mr & Mrs Lupel

I always want to express my gratitude for the help you're giving me. Though due when lies on you to answer specific questions in the recent past, I have still relied on the thoughtful decision making processes I have developed. This development is in large part due to you Mr Lupel.

I am grateful to both of you for always making me comfortable in your home and also being thoughtful, dignified people whom I view as models for myself. Thank you both and I'll talk to you soon.

Sincerely,

Dear Warren,

Many thanks for all your efforts on my behalf. Things are coming together for us.

We could not have managed without you, and it will always be grateful.

Sincerely,

Basic

Dear Warren

This is late coming but please accept my deepest appreciation and heartfelt thanks for your help in the Debbie Santiago case.

I am very grateful to you and Mike Weininger for doing all you did in a sad situation. I know Debbie is extremely grateful as well.

Warren you are truly a good person and someone I proudly can call my friend.

Kenny Jablonski

be grateful.

Sincerely,

Bonnie

Dear Warren,

Many thanks for all your efforts on our behalf. Things are coming together for us.

We could not have managed without you, and I will always

1-30-04

Dear Warren,

This is late coming but please accept my deepest appreciation and heartfelt thanks for your help in the Debbie Santiago case.

I am very grateful to you and Mike Weininger for doing all you did in a sad situation. I know Debbie is extremely grateful as well,

Warren, you are truly a good person and someone I proudly can call my friend. Kenny Jablonski

21

Dear Warren,

I've been meaning to drop you a live ever since I learned of your involvement in the alotoor case. Like the rest of the public, I'm feeling a little whiplashed by this bizarre case. Nonetheless, what has continued to keep me in gary's alotoor's corner is not Cornwell Crowell stead, but Warren Hupel, whose own high standards of integrity are more than familiar to me. I am sure this has been a nightmare for you, and I do hope you'll try to take a breather. I can't afford to lose a dammed good attorney to a heart attack.

7859B South shores In clge Coyws

Warmest regards,

Ian Me Reynolds

May Your Holiday

be

Heavenly

May god bless you in everything that you do. Thank you!!! You were my savior.

You were my savior.

Always,

Elena N. Duarte

Dear Warren,

I've been meaning to drop you a line ever since I learned of your involvement in the Dotson case. Like the rest of the public, I'm feeling a little whiplashed by this bizarre case. Nonetheless, what has continued to keep me in Gary Dotson's corner is not Cathleen Crowell Webb, but Warren Lupel, whose own high standards of integrity are more than familiar to me. I'm sure this has been a nightmare for you, and I do hope you'll try to take a breather. I can't afford to lose a damned good attorney to a heart attack.

Warmest regards,
Jan McReynolds

7859 B South Shore Dr.
Chgo. 60649

May your Holiday be Heavenly

May God bless you in everything that you do. Thank you!!!
You were my savior.

Always,
Elena N. Duarte

23

Dear Warren,

You are an extraordinary lawyer and an unusually generous soul. I am grateful for the privilege of calling you my friend.

Love

Dear Mr. Hupel,

Thank you from the bottom of my heart for helping me pay for my mother's funeral. I hope to see you in person sometime soon.

Love Scott

June 11, 2004

Dear Warren,

You are an extraordinary lawyer and an unusually generous soul. I am grateful for the privilege of calling you my friend.

Love, Bruce

Dear Mr Lupel,

Thank you from the Bottom of my Heart for helping me Pay for my mothers funeral. I Hope to See you in Person Some time Soon.

Love Scott

Dear Warren,

A hearty thank you for your efforts on my behalf. Your presence, stature, and involvement brought credibility to our case and assisted greatly in bringing this matter to a satisfactory conclusion.

I appreciate the personal touch of inviting me to your home for a delicious meal and good conversation. Please extend my thoughts to Sally.

You and Jeff are a formidable team and I will be forever grateful for the manner in which you represented my interests.

Sincerely,

Dear Warren,

I hope all is well. I just wanted to thank you again for all of your help and guidance both through my problems with the immigration practice and again with the winding up of my law practice. Your advice was extremely helpful and following it surely kept me from getting myself in trouble. You have long been and continue to be a role model & what and attorney should be. All is well with me. I love my new career. Have a happy and healthy year. Fred

12-28-00

Dear Warren,

A hearty Thank You for your efforts on my behalf. Your presence, stature, and involvement brought credibility to our case and assisted greatly in bringing this matter to a satisfactory conclusion.

I appreciate the personal touch of inviting me to your home for a delicious meal and good conversation. Please extend my thanks to Sally.

You and Jeff are a formidable team and I will be forever grateful for the manner in which you represented my interests. Sincerely,

Dear Warren,

I hope all is well. I just wanted to thank you again for all of your help and guidance both through my problems with the immigration practice and again with the winding up of my law practice. Your advise was extremely helpful and following it surely kept me from getting myself in trouble. You have long been and continue to be a role model of what an attorney should be. All is well with me. I love my new career. Have a happy and healthy year. Fred

Dear Sonny,

There and many things to thank you for and you're always doing more. Thank you for being the kind and generous man that you are. Thank you from the bottom of my heart for everything you have done.

Love,

WARREN-

Thank you again for your time & advise and for going with me AROL on Monday. I greatly appreciate your assistance and hopefully that will be the end of it. I also greatly appreciated your refuse to accept payment for your time spent with me.

I know of your reputation for doing wonderful for Pro-Bond work, but I never imagined or expected to be the recipient of your services. Please accept a small token of Kathy's & my deep appreciation- Steve said you seemed to like this, So please enjoy it with our heartfelt thanks.

Dear Sonny,   2/3/02

There are so many things to thank you for
And you're always doing more. Thank you
for being the kind and generous man
that you are. Thank you from the
bottom of my heart for everything you
have done.

                    Love,
                    Kathie

WARREN -

    THANK YOU AGAIN FOR YOUR TIME &
ADVISE AND FOR GOING WITH ME TO THE
PROC ON MONDAY - I GREATLY APPRECIATE
YOUR ASSISTANCE AND HOPEFULLY THAT
WILL BE THE END OF IT. I ALSO GREATLY
APPRECIATED YOUR REFUSAL TO ACCEPT
PAYMENT FOR YOUR TIME SPENT WITH ME.
I KNOW OF YOUR REPUTATION FOR DOING
WONDERFUL PRO BONO WORK, BUT I NEVER
IMAGINED OR EXPECTED TO BE THE RECIPIENT
OF YOUR SERVICES - PLEASE ACCEPT A SMALL
TOKEN OF KATHY'S & MY DEEP APPRECIATION - STEVE
SAID YOU SEEMED TO LIKE THIS, SO PLEASE
ENJOY IT WITH OUR HEARTFELT THANKS

To,

Mr Hupel,

Thank you for making all this possible

From 6-16-75

From: Mr Hendricks

&

Daughter Devendaly Hendricks

Ps- Thanks again

To:
Mr. Lupel,

Thank you for making

* all this Possible.
Prom: 6-16-75

From: Mrs. Hendricks

&

Daughter Gwendolyn
Hendricks

Ps-Thanks Again

Augie Mass

Attorney At Law

Warren-

I will always remember the help you gave me. Thank you. I hope all is well. Let's get together some time.

Augie

Law Offices of Augustus F. Mass

1515 Sherldan Road, suite 23 Wilmette, Illinois 60091

Tel: 312 636 4611 Fax: 312 873 3879

amoss@mosslewoffices.com

Augie Moss

Attorney At Law

Warren —
I will always remember
the help you gave me.
Thank you. I hope all
is well. Lets get together
some time.
Augie

Law Offices of Augustus F. Moss

1515 Sheridan Road, Suite 23   Wilmette, Illinois 60091
Tel: 312.636.4611   Fax: 312.873.3879
amoss@mosslawoffices.com

Warren,

I won't ever be able to thank you enough for your support and encouragement over the years. You've been a mentor, friend, etc. and you are a big part of the award I received.

Tanti braziel

Franco

Warren -

I won't ever be able to thank you enough for your support and encouragement over the years. You've been a mentor, friend, etc and you are a big part of the award I received!

Tanti Grazie!

Franco

Dear Warren,

Just a note to congratulate you on your award for distinguished services to law & society. You have long brought honor to our profession and I count myself blessed to be your friend. Hope to see you at the breakdesk.

Mick

Contact information

847-919-088 (cou)

847-869-0258 (home)

Jmn353enyu.edu

Joequelinenew3ead.com

Mr Hupel,

Thank you is not enough but it's all I know.. You have been a huge blessing in my life! From mock trial to giving me a job you have been a big part of my high school career. Thank you for giving me the chance to work for you. This job is such a big deal for me I learned so much and I got to meet so many different people…This has been a wonderful summer and mostly because of you. Thank you for this great opportunity. If you ever need anyone/ if you ever have room for me I would love to come back to work for you on breaks or in the summer. Thank you so much Mr Hupel for everything.

-Joequelinene M Neone

11/16/10

DEAR WARREN,

Just a Note to Congratulate you on your Award For Distinguished Service to Law & Society. You have long brought honor to our Profession And I count myself blessed to be your Friend. Hope to see you at the Breakfast

Mick

Contact information
847-914-0818 (cell)
847-869-0258 (home)
JMA353@nyu.edu
Jacquelinenewse@aol.com } email

Mr Lupel,

Thank you is not enough, but its all I know... you have been a huge blessing in my life! From mock-mal to giving me a job you have been a big part of my high school career. Thank you for giving me the chance to work for you. This job is such a big deal for me I learned so much and I got to meet so many different people... This has been a wonderful summer and mostly because of you. Thank you for this great opportunity. If you ever need anyone / if you have room for me I would love to come back to work for you on breaks or in the summer. Thank you so much Mr Lupel for everything — Jacqueline M. Newsone

37

Warren,

I cannot thank you enough for all that you have done for me. Two years ago I walked into your office with no clue what it meant to be a lawyer. Your Mentoring, guidance and friendship has taught me it is much more than past draftine pleadings and making court appearances. You have taught me how to think, act and present myself like a lawyer, and for that I thank you.

I admire everything you stand for. I have always been impressed how so many people in the legal community know and respect you. At first, I thought it was because you were a great lawyer, but over two years I have realized it is also because you are such a great person.

You did not have to hire me, let me handle cases, give me a raise when Lisa lost her job, wrote my name as an "associate" in the Sullivan's law directory, give me selfless advice about lawyer job opportunities or bring me to Springfield for your supreme court hearing. You did not have to do any of things… But you did and I will never forget it.

I am leaving Lupez Wenninger LLP a young, confident lawyer and I owe it all to you. Thank you. Sincerely,

Peter Lapin

Warren,

I cannot thank you enough for all that you
ive done for me. Two years ago I walked into
our office with no clue what it meant to
be a lawyer. Your mentoring, guidance and
friendship has taught me it is much more than
just drafting pleadings and making court appearances.
You have taught me how to think, act and present
myself like a lawyer, and for that I thank you.

I admire everything you stand for. I have
always been impressed how so many people in the
legal community know and respect you. At first,
I thought it was because you were a great

lawyer, but over two years I have
realized it is also because you are such a
great person.

You did not have to hire me, let me handle
cases, give me a raise when Lisa lost her job,
put my name as an "associate" in the Sullivan's
Law Directory, give me selfless advice about
other job opportunities or bring me to
Kingfield for your supreme court hearing.
You did not have to do any of things... but
you did and I will never forget it.

I am leaving Luper Weininger LLP a
young, confident lawyer and I owe it
all to you. Thank you.

                    Sincerely,
                    Peter Lapin

Warren,

Thank you so much for everything you did for me from taking me off ledge the ledge when I got the job letter, to your thoughtful edits of my written response, to your guiding rich and use step by step through the hearing process (we were both amazed at how accurate your predictions were).

This was not a pleasant experience but at least it reminded me that there are still good people in the world.

Gratefully,

Kevin.

Because your always there when I need you

Warren,

Thanks so much for everything you did for me—from talking me off the ledge when I got the JIB letter, to your thoughtful edits of my written response, to your guiding Rich and me step by step through the hearing process (we were both amazed at how accurate your predictions were).

This was not a pleasant experience but at least it reminded me that there are still good people in the world.

Gratefully,

Kevin

Because your always there when I need you.

P.S. my wife Laura sends her regards

June 23, 2016

Dear Warren,

Over the past six years your tough questions and generosity of spirit have made LTF a strong organization.

We are grateful for your friendship and support.

With best wishes,

Mark David.

Sharon

P.S. my wife Laura
Sent her regards.

June 23, 2016

Dear Warren,

Over the past six years
your tough questions and
generosity of spirit have made
LT7 a stronger organization.
We are grateful for your friendship
and support.

With best wishes,

Mark

David

Sharon

43

Thanks
for going there.

Warren,

Thank you for your help. Enclosed please find a check for you. My first dollars practicing again. I am honored to be your friend. The transition is a little difficult but business will be on heck soon.

Your friends, Peter Whitrop

7-18-08

Thanks
for going there.

WARREN,

THANK YOU FOR YOUR HELP.
ENCLOSED PLEASE FIND A CHECK
FOR $100. MY FIRST DOLLARS
PRACTICING AGAIN. I AM HONORED
TO BE YOUR FRIEND. THE TRANSITION
IS a little difficult BUT BUSINESS
WILL BE ON track SOON.

YOUR FRIEND, Peter Winthrop

10/29/93

Dear Warren,

I want to sincerely thank you for all your help & support. You have renewed my faith in mankind-although I'll always be hesitant and & certainly are cautious when it comes to dealing with many. The focus of my life is no longer this incredible & my owner is annoying.

I'll there saw anything I can do for you or you drive in the area of commercial training of consulting, please let me please.

Once again, "thank you".

3/9/11

Dear Warren,

On the road of life,

It's not where you go

But who you are with

That makes the difference

Thanks for letting me tag along

Your

Happy Anniversary!

Love you

Marilyn

10/29/93

Dear Warren,

    I want to sincerely thank you for all your help & support. You have renewed my faith in mankind — although I'll always be hesitant & cautious who I confide in when it comes to dealing with others. The fear of my life is no longer this "incident" & my career is progressing.

    If there's ever anything I can do for you or your firm in the area of communication training or consulting, please let me know.

    Once again, "thank you."

             Best wishes, [signature]

3/9/11

Dear Warren,

    On the road of life,
    it's not where you go
    but who you're with
    that makes the difference.

    Thanks for letting me tag along.

           40th
    Happy Anniversary!

           Love you
           Marilyn

47

7-18-08

Hi Warren,

Here's to you!

Congratulations

1968-2008

40 years in law

You have elevated the profession I am honored to have been a client.

Your friend,

Geta Winkling

Dear Mr Hupel,

like saying "thank you"

to someone as nice as you!

From helping to try and solve the problem with IRS.

U were fiver for get what you done

God bless you always and I will always remember you in my prayer

God bless

Ernistine

7-18-08

HI WARREN,

here's to you!

congratulations

1968 - 2008

40 YEARS IN
LAW

YOU HAVE
ELEVATED THE
PROFESSION AND I AM
HONORED TO HAVE BEEN A CLIENT

YOUR FRIEND,
Peta Winfred

Dear Mr. Jupel

...like saying "thank you"
to someone as nice as you!
for helping to try and solve
the problem with IRS
I will never for get you done
God Bless You always and I will
Always remember you in my prayers
God Bless
Ernestine

You know-

If you keep having this

Things you've going to get old

Warren,

I really don't know what to say at this point. You have become so much to me. I mean in truly contemplating myself, my identity is partly how strong I identify w/you.

A number of people have commented that you and I are a lot alike. My avg hope is that I continue to develop and became so fine a person as how you are.

P. S.

I owe you a bunch

Tory Gigs

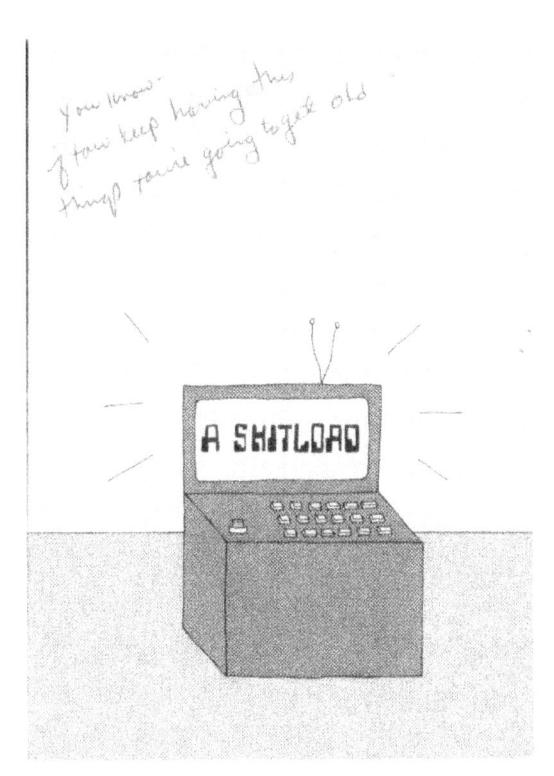

Warren,

Congrats on your ISBA fellowship award!

It will be a great event only because the award recipient is you!

God bless, Keep will always fondly,

12/2/10

Warren,

Congrats on your ISBA
Fellowship Award!
It will be a great event only
because the award recipient is

You!

God Bless, Keep Well Always,
Fondly, YB

12/2/10

Dear Warren,

And succeeded,
Congratulations1

So very happy for you!
You are so deserving…
you pillar of the community, you!

Loius

Dear Warren,

and succeeded,

Congratulations!

So very happy for you!
You are so deserving... you pillar
of the community (you)!

Gloria

My DADDY
IS THE
BEST!

From the daddy picking!
company! Love aliso

MY DADDY IS THE BEST!

from the dad-
dy picking!
company! love
alison

Friday

Dear Sonny

I am raw sitting in our yard "summing" myself & meet het to scriddle this note to you to and to your "fan" mail.

I feel like a fool sitting here doddling while lecturing to your compassionate plea.

Have if curse been following the case-not only because of suu but due to my belief in dariy's innocent.

Just want to pay raw proud I am to know and be able to call you a friend!

Whatever the situation-you should certainly be proud of your efforts.

Big love to you, you See the like Either you celebrate your victory, lets hear from you,

Sonny again congratulations regardless the outcome-take care of yourself now as the storm has been tremendous.

Much love

Sande Selwenz

Friday

Dear Sonny -

I am now sitting in our yard "sunning" myself & just had to scribble this note to you to add to your "fan" mail.

I feel like a fool sitting here actually sobbing while listening to your compassionate plea.

I've of course been following the case - not only because of you - but due to my belief in Gary's innocence.

Just want to say how proud I am to know you & be able to call you a friend!

Whatever the outcome - you should certainly be proud of your efforts.

My love to you, Sally & the kids. After you celebrate your VICTORY, let's hear from you.

Sonny again, congratulations regardless of the outcome - take care of yourself now as the strain has been tremendous.

Much love,
Sande Schwartz

59

2/25

Dear Warren,

I know I should have contacted you earlier, but I procrastinated. This is a thank you letter because you helped me more than you know! Because of your motivation I gained self confidence in myself when taking my last semester finals. I increased my guide point average a whole grade from a 1.9 to a 2.85. Although my cumulative average is only a 2.33. At least I know that I can finish my education.

Warren, you gave me the best advice, when I met with you during the summer to study the noun topics fast and how the material relates to curse topics. Everything fell into place, for me after that. I don't know how to thank you but I am so lucky to know that I can rely on you for help Thank you for everything.

Love,

Katherine Amari

2/25 Dear Warren,

I knew I should have contacted you earlier, but I procrastinated. This is a thank you letter because you helped me more than you know! Because of your instruction, I gained self-confidence in myself when taking my last semester finals. I increased my grade-point average a whole grade (from a 1.9 to a 2.85). Although my cumulative average is only a 2.53, at least I know that I can finish my education.

Warren, you gave me the best advice when I met with you during the summer, to study the main topics first and how the material relates to these topics. Everything fell into place for me after that. I don't know how to thank you, but I am so lucky to know that I can rely on you for help. Thank you for everything.

Love,
Katherine Amari

61

3rd Feb, 97

Dear Warren,

Please accept my deep appreciation for your guidance regarding my various situations, you are one of a kind friend. While I don't have a clue as to how it will all work out, what I do know and will never forget is that you were the only one genuinely cared. Your willingness to give, will I am sure never ever for then by these you have befriended.

I remember once while we were discussing mutual friends, with a stern (Almost Demanding) voice you said "Friends don't keep score "you paused then continued "How could they". I had the feeling that you were actually astonished that it could be any other way, how innocent I thought, for a guy who has been hurt, even by friends. Later as I was rethinking your statement I realized, It wasn't innocent's at all, it was provocative almost religious, beneficiary on insane expectations of others, or was I?" Warren, the score us ten-zip in your favor (or mine, depending how you look at it) but it's only the second quarter, I am still capable of a few bombs and if necessary A Hale Marry

Thanks for being my friend.

Donald

3rd Feb, 97

Dear Warren

Please accept my deep appreciation for your guidance regarding my various situations, you are a one-of-a-kind friend. While I don't have a clue as to how it will all work out, what I do know and will never forget is that you were the only one who genuinely cared. Your willingness to give, will I'm sure never ever be forgotten by those you have befriended. I remember once while we were discussing mutual friends, with a stern (almost demanding) voice you said "Friends don't keep score" you paused then continued "How could they". I had the feeling that you were actually astonished that it could be any other way, how innocent I thought, for a guy who has been hurt, even by friends. Later as I was rethinking your statement I realized, it wasn't innocence at all, it was provocative almost religious, boardering on insane expectations of others, or was it? Warren, the score is Ten-Zip in your favor (or mine depending how you look at it) but its only the second quarter, I'm still capable of a few bombs and if necessary a Hale Mary. Thanks for being my friend.   Donald

63

Mr Gibbs

Enclosed are the letters/notes which I am hopeful that you can compile in to a book or other type of compilation e.g album (3 copies)

I view this as a difficult task. I removed all envelopes and reduced the total number by at least one half.

Look forward to hearing from you.

Warren Lupel

847-602-0524

Sent from Gmail Mobile

Mr. Gibbs

Enclosed are the letters/notes which I am hopeful that you can compile in to a book or other type of compilation e.g. album (3copies)

I view this as a difficult task. I removed all envelopes and reduced the total number by at least one half.

Look forward to hearing from you

Warren Lupel
847-602-0524

Sent from Gmail Mobile

Deane B. Brown

Dear Warren,

Before I leave Katz Randall, I want to thank you for a great 4+ years of practicing law together. It has been a pleasure and a privilege to be your partner. I truly appreciate that you have been supportive of me and my professional development. I have learned so much from working with you, especially in the professional responsibility area. I look forward to our continued friendship and working relationship on our few outstanding cedeo. Thank you for everything. Yours truly,

Deane

Deane B. Brown

8/30

Dear Warren,

Before I leave Katz Randall, I want to thank you for a great 4+ years of practicing law together. It has been a pleasure and a privilege to be your partner. I truly appreciate that you have always been supportive of me and my professional development. I have learned so much from working with you, especially in the professional responsibility area. I look forward to our continued friendship and working relationship on our few outstanding cases. Thanks again for everything. Yours truly,

Deane

Youshine

Warren, thank you so much for being an amazing friend and advocate for Brendon. We don't often get mentors with as much relevant experience as you, and I am so glad we can use cell those skills you came with to help these boys who haven't often had any worthwhile male role models. I know your life is already very full with family and travel. I am so thankful that you've chosen to spend your free time with us.

Thank you for everything,

and happy volunteer week!

-Vera

Warren, thank you so much for being an amazing friend and advocate for Brenden. We don't often get mentors with as much relevant experience as you, and I'm so glad we can use all those skills you come with to help those boys who haven't often had any worthwhile male role models. I know your life is already very full with family and travel — I am so thankful that you've chosen to spend your free time with us.

Thank you for everything, and happy Volunteer Week!

— Vera

Dear Warren,

Thank you so very much for your kindness, time and laugh. I am must grateful. Thank you for hearing and sut when I needed someone to talk to so desperately.

Ivary, you blew from sow daeve and repay saw a thousand fold.

Thank again.

Sincerely,

3680

Dear Mr. Engel,

Thank you so very much for
your kindness, time & help.
I'm most grateful. Thank you for
helping me out when I needed
someone to talk to so desperately.

May God Bless you & yours
and repay you a thousand fold.
Thanks again

Sincerely

Josephine F. Bromberg

Dr. Karen L. Jaffe

Suite 607

30 North Michigan Avernue

Chicago, lasota 60602

(312) 263-1760

to thank you for your remos reprend der ty be of axy Alsvice to fore please it me riturates favor

it would be a pleasure meet you at some point unereter my legal matters. take me to mit a lacy uuta a mese uno bul

always he thought of as a menschiﻣﻊ my mind.

Sincerely,

Karen Jaffe

Dr. Karen L. Jaffe
Suite 607
30 North Michigan Avenue
Chicago, Illinois 60602
(312) 263-1780

to thank you for your
enormous help and generously
of time. If I can be of any
service to you please let me
return the favor.

It would be a pleasure to
meet you at some point,
wherever my legal matters
take me, to put a face
with a man who will
always be thought of as
a "mensch" in my mind.

Sincerely,
Karen Jaffe

From the desk of

RICHARD CAIPANO

Suite 725

20 North Clark Street

Tel (312) 346 0570

Fax (312) 782-0156

2 APRIL 2008

Chicago Illinois 60602

Warren,

You are truly a Lowyork Lawyer- the brightest compliment ONE may accord a colleque. I am blessed by my friends and doubly blessed when you who I wumbe Among them jumps into the Lesun to protect that which Is denpast to me -my integrity.

Thank You AGNIN AGAINs

From the Desk of

RICHARD CAIFANO

SUITE 725
20 NORTH CLARK STREET
CHICAGO, ILLINOIS 60602

TEL. (312) 346-0570
FAX (312) 782-0156

2 APRIL 2008

WARREN,

You are truly a LAWYER'S LAWYER — the highest compliment one may accord a colleague. I am blessed by my friends and doubly blessed when you — who I number among them — jumps into the arena to protect that which is dearest to me — my integrity.

THANK YOU
AGAIN + AGAIN

Dr. Karen L. Jaffe

Suite 607

30 North Michigan Avenue

Chicago, hmnts 00002

(312) 203-1780

1/27/000

Dear Warren,

Considering tea roll you played en FRE coussey my legal indvers and emotional stat, unes noll is overdue. I wanted to chauk you for your willingness to share your earned, enngolfiel, bicid mousut my stutation. additinally, your candor regarding the gentlemen ung beamivaly dramatics as you gathered my poor choice of husband was been complicasta prakty both bydswing lavits bad and luck pidges with at any rute, I wanted

referred I me to you, en Hanky idined cudibility wicth me. To say wat way you were a macun In a storm although

Dr. Karen L. Jaffe
Suite 607
30 North Michigan Avenue
Chicago, Illinois 60602
(312) 263-1780

1/27/06

Dear Warren,

Considering the role you played in the course of my legal matters and emotional state, this note is overdue. I wanted to thank you for your willingness to share your learned, insightful, lucid thoughts on my situation. Additionally, your candor regarding the gentlemen who referred me to you, instantly earned credibility with me.

To say that you were a "beacon in a storm" although seemingly dramatic, is quite appropos. As you gathered my poor choice of husband has been complicated greatly by dealing bad luck with both lawyers and judges.

At any rate, I wanted

Warren

You have been selected to receive the Arving Biyer award for 1982. The family does not pret the award back year. Your Jeans Eve Party Park is given to that has bem a steadfast friend under the presenen fo Capitalit society.

Wanen Lupel Har reputation in the Community a for loyalty, integrity anal hemen warnth. Many indubbel benefil from A skilled mind Keen businen senary

12/31/82

Warren:

You have been selected to receive the Irving Beyer award for 1982. The family does not present the award each year. The "New Years Eve Party Pack" is given to an individual that has been a steadfast friend under the pressure of our capitalist society.

Warren Lupel has a reputation in the community for loyalty, integrity, and human warmth. Many individuals benefit from a skilled mind and a keen business sense,

79

very few combine that advantage with an understay of people and an ability love unselfiskly. Best of lealth and good huna for 1983

Love

Respondent

By Phil Aya

very few combine that
advantage with an understanding
of people and an ability
to love unselfishly.
    Best of health
and good humor for
1983

            Love

        Respondent
        By Phil Byr

the court.

Reception to boost new Lupel fund

By JOHN FLYNN ROONEY

Laws w

The Illinois Bar Foundation is spon- soring a reception to benefit a fund aimed at providing assistance to lawyers who cannot practice because of itness or other disabilities.

The fund is named for Warren Lapel. a partner with Weinberg, Richmond LLP who is a "Gold Fellow of the Bar Foun dation and an ex officio board member He served as the foundation's president for two years ending in late 2004.

The Warres Lepel Fund was created last year to supplement the foundation's subsistence program by providing finan- cial aid to lawyers experiencing diffical ties because of serious illness, such as

"I've been working for some time to create a meaningful fund for this specific purpose," Lapel said. "This purpose, to the best of my knowledge, is not addressed by any other foundation or charity in this state."

One of Lupel's clients made a anony mous gift of $25,000 in seed money as a tribute to Lapel's leadership of the foun dation

The client "really wanted to say thank you to Warren in a special way," said Susan M. Pierson, the Bar Foundation's executive director

The Bar Foundation currently pro vides monthly subsistence checks to five eligible Illinois lawyers, Pierson added. Often, lawyers beset by illness or dis ability face losing their homes, she said.

"We're trying to provide them an opportunity to live [within] reasonable means," Pierson said.

Continued from page 3

Sole practitioners who have inade- quate or no insurance and who lack retirement plans are particularly vulner able when catastrophe strikes, Lapel said.

The Lapel Fund is designed to "create an endowment from which investment or interest revenue can be used on a per- petual basis to assist hwyers or their families" in case of severe financial diff culties, Lapel said.

The fund-raising event will be held from 5 to 7 pm, March 29, t the Union League Club, 65 W Jackson Blvd in Chicago. The event initially was to be held at a downtown law firm but, due to Reception-page 24

a significant response, was moved to a larger space, Pierson noted.

Individual tickets cost $100, while a host committee will pay $1,000 and a friends committee $500. Ticket requests the court.

Reception to boost new Lupel fund

By JOHN FLYNN ROONEY
Law Bulletin staff writer

The Illinois Bar Foundation is sponsoring a reception to benefit a fund aimed at providing assistance to lawyers who cannot practice because of illness or other disabilities.

The fund is named for Warren Lupel, a partner with Weinberg, Richmond LLP, who is a "Gold Fellow" of the Bar Foundation and an ex officio board member. He served as the foundation's president for two years ending in late 2004.

The Warren Lupel Fund was created last year to supplement the foundation's subsistence program by providing financial aid to lawyers experiencing difficulties because of serious illness, such as cancer.

"I've been working for some time to create a meaningful fund for this specific purpose," Lupel said. "This purpose, to the best of my knowledge, is not addressed by any other foundation or charity in this state."

One of Lupel's clients made an anonymous gift of $25,000 in seed money as a tribute to Lupel's leadership of the foundation.

The client "really wanted to say thank you to Warren in a special way," said Susan M. Pierson, the Bar Foundation's executive director.

The Bar Foundation currently provides monthly subsistence checks to five eligible Illinois lawyers, Pierson added. Often, lawyers beset by illness or disability face losing their homes, she said.

"We're trying to provide them an opportunity to live [within] reasonable means," Pierson said.

Sole practitioners who have inadequate or no insurance and who lack retirement plans are particularly vulnerable when catastrophe strikes, Lupel said.

The Lupel Fund is designed to "create an endowment from which investment or interest revenue can be used on a perpetual basis to assist lawyers or their families" in case of severe financial difficulties, Lupel said.

The fund-raising event will be held from 5 to 7 p.m., March 29, at the Union League Club, 65 W. Jackson Blvd. in Chicago. The event initially was to be held at a downtown law firm but, due to

Reception — page 24

Continued from page 3

a significant response, was moved to a larger space, Pierson noted.

Individual tickets cost $100, while a host committee will pay $1,000 and a friends committee $500. Ticket requests

March 21, 2005

Warren Lupel, Esq

Weinberg Richmond, LLP

333 W Wacker Drive Suite 1800

Chicago, IL 60606-1288

Dear Warren

The purpose of this letter is to just congratulate you on the fantastic turn-out in connection with the Warren Lupe Fund Nobody is more deserving of those results than you. I think that it is a measure of how well respected and appreciated you are throughout the community.

I can personally say that you have been very generous with your time in the past and that too is a measure of what a great lawyer and humanitarian you are

I won't be able to make the fundraiser on March 29" because I will be in Florida with my wife and daughters I have however made a contribution to the fund and I feel privileged to support you in that endeavor.

I hope to see you in Canada in the Summer, although some conflicts are arising because now it seems that other members of my family would like to join in on the trip, including my ten year old daughter, and I think that we are running out of capacity at the Birch Island Lodge. We see what happens, but in the meantime, congratulations and I hope that you enjoy your evening with all of those who admire and respect you Rest assured that I will be there in spirit

and being

Very truly yours.

ABF im

Anthony B. Ferraro Attorney at Law

Thanks waren

any

THE LAW OFFICES OF

ANTHONY B. FERRARO
5600 NORTH RIVER ROAD
SUITE 188 764
ROSEMONT, ILLINOIS 60018-5166
www.abferrarolaw.com
email: abfcpalaw@aol.com
(847) 292-1220
(847) 292-1821 FAX

ANTHONY B. FERRARO
ATTORNEY - CPA
OF COUNSEL:
LEONARD F. AMARI
JOSEPH F. LOCALLO, JR
BRUNO J. TASSONE

ADDITIONAL OFFICE LOCATIONS
BY APPOINTMENT ONLY:
- CHICAGO LOOP
- GURNEE, ILLINOIS
- LIBERTYVILLE, ILLINOIS
- LAKE FOREST, ILLINOIS

March 21, 2006

Warren Lupel, Esq.
Weinberg Richmond, LLP
333 W Wacker Drive
Suite 1800
Chicago, IL 60606-1288

Dear Warren:

The purpose of this letter is to just congratulate you on the fantastic turn-out in connection with the Warren Lupel Fund. Nobody is more deserving of those results than you. I think that it is a measure of how well respected and appreciated you are throughout the community.

I can personally say that you have been very generous with your time in the past and that too is a measure of what a great lawyer and humanitarian you are.

I won't be able to make the fundraiser on March 29th because I will be in Florida with my wife and daughters. I have however made a contribution to the fund and I feel privileged to support you in that endeavor.

I hope to see you in Canada in the Summer, although some conflicts are arising because now it seems that other members of my family would like to join in on the trip, including my ten year old daughter, and I think that we are running out of capacity at the Birch Island Lodge. We'll see what happens, but in the meantime, congratulations and I hope that you enjoy your evening with all of those who admire and respect you.

Rest assured that I will be there in spirit and being.

Very truly yours,

Anthony B. Ferraro
Attorney at Law

ABF:lm

C:\wpdocs\Clientco 05\lupel.ltr

87

DAVIS FRIEDMAN

Larry Kane, Partner Landevisfied.com

March 24, 2005

Warren Lupel, E

333 W. Wacker Drive

Suite 1800

Chicago, Illinois 60606

Dear Warren

Congratulations on the creation of the Warren Lupel Fund and the honors the Illinois Bar Foundation are granting to you. I've always known you've been a good guy.

Our firm is making a donation in your honor, so you won't be getting a separate donation from me. And, as much as I'd like to be present, I would much rather be out of town on vacation with my wife, which I will be.

So, you'll have to settle for my taking you to lunch sometime in April. I'll call you after I return. Congratulations, again.

Cordially,

Larry R.Ran

Larry R. Kine

LRK/dm

DAVIS|FRIEDMAN

Davis Friedman Zavett Kane MacRae Marcus Rubens LLP | 135 S. LaSalle Street, 36th Floor | Chicago IL 60603 | T 312 782 2220 F 312 782 0464 | www.davisfriedman.com

Larry R. Kane, Partner | Lkane@davisfriedman.com

March 24, 2005

Warren Lupel, Esq.
333 W. Wacker Drive
Suite 1800
Chicago, Illinois 60606

Dear Warren:

Congratulations on the creation of the Warren Lupel Fund and the honors the Illinois Bar Foundation are granting to you. I've always known you've been a good guy.

Our firm is making a donation in your honor, so you won't be getting a separate donation from me. And, as much as I'd like to be present, I would much rather be out of town on vacation with my wife, which I will be.

So, you'll have to settle for my taking you to lunch sometime in April. I'll call you after I return.

Congratulations, again.

Cordially,

Larry R. Kane

LRK/dm

LAW OFFICES

Komie And ASSOCIATES

One North LaSalle Street - Suite 4200

Сыстро. Шина 10602-4005 Celephone (312) 263-2800 www.komie-and-associates.com

March 11, 2005

Stephen M. Komic

Elizabeth P. Butler

Darius R. Dirmantas

Brian C. King

Debra A. Liss

Elisabeth A. Ritter

OF COUNSEL

Mark B. Belokon

Marc D. Welfe

InvescioACOR

Paul J. Cieline

Warren Lupel, Esq.

Katz Randall Weinberg & Richmond

333 W. Wacker Drive, Suite 1800 Chicago, Illinois 60606

Re: The Warren Lupel Fund

Dear Warren:

Congratulations on being the inspiration for the creation of "The Warren Lupel Fund." which will provide aid to dependent members of the Bar. I cannot think of a person who has exhibited greater qualities of charity towards the disabled members of our profession. If memory serves me correctly, I recall discussing with you the first disabled member of the bar I ever met. Larry Cohen.

The decision of the Board of Directors of the Illinois Bar Foundation to cast the fund in your name and honor will hopefully lead to a significant commitment by the Bar Foundation to the unfortunate members who suffer from mental disease or physical illness during their careers.

I regret I'm unable to attend the celebration in your honor on March 29 at the Union League Club. I am scheduled to take depositions in San Francisco, California with Rico Mirabelli in a case which is set for a hearing on April 1" here in Chicago. Should circumstances change, I would be more than happy to go there and cheer you on. Otherwise, know I'm there in spirit wishing you all the best.

Very truly yours,

KOMIE AND ASSOCIATES

Sleptin Kamie

Stephen M. Komie

SMK/jn

LAW OFFICES

KOMIE AND ASSOCIATES
One North LaSalle Street - Suite 4200
Chicago, Illinois 60602-4005
Telephone (312) 263-2800
www.komie-and-associates.com

Stephen M. Komie
Elizabeth D. Butler
Darius R. Dirmantas
Brian E. King
Debra A. Liss
Elisabeth A. Ritter

of counsel
Mark B. Beloken
Marc D. Wolfe

investigator
Paul J. Ciolino

March 11, 2005

Warren Lupel, Esq.
Katz Randall Weinberg & Richmond
333 W. Wacker Drive, Suite 1800
Chicago, Illinois 60606

Re: The Warren Lupel Fund

Dear Warren:

Congratulations on being the inspiration for the creation of "The Warren Lupel Fund," which will provide aid to dependent members of the Bar. I cannot think of a person who has exhibited greater qualities of charity towards the disabled members of our profession. If memory serves me correctly, I recall discussing with you the first disabled member of the bar I ever met, Larry Cohen.

The decision of the Board of Directors of the Illinois Bar Foundation to cast the fund in your name and honor will hopefully lead to a significant commitment by the Bar Foundation to the unfortunate members who suffer from mental disease or physical illness during their careers.

I regret I'm unable to attend the celebration in your honor on March 29th at the Union League Club. I am scheduled to take depositions in San Francisco, California with Rico Mirabelli in a case which is set for a hearing on April 1st here in Chicago. Should circumstances change, I would be more than happy to go there and cheer you on. Otherwise, know I'm there in spirit wishing you all the best.

Very truly yours,

KOMIE AND ASSOCIATES

Stephen M. Komie

SMK/jn

92

Illinois Bar Journal; October 2000

Bar Journal

Letters to the Editor

Laurels for a laureate

Editor:

For several years I have been fortunate to know Warren Lupel, the laureate of the month of the Academy of Illinois Lawyers, and consider him a friend. Tom Johnson's moving portrait in the August issue, in the short space available, shows that it does more honor to the Academy to have Warren as a Laureate than vice versa. I am reminded that it is "far beyond our poor powers to add or detract" to his lifetime of service.

While it is certainly possible, as space permits, to add many additional features to Tom's tribute (but not enhance his eloquence), such as Warren's service with the Illinois Bar Foundation to name just one, the best way I can think to phrase it is that Warren Lupel makes me proud to be a lawyer.

-Phillip B. Lenzini

East Peoria, IL

Readers of the Journal are invited to submit short letters, preferably not exceeding 500 words, expressing their opinions, or giving information, as to any matter appearing in the Journal or otherwise. The editor reserves the right to select the communications or excerpts therefrom to publish and to edit for grammar and style. The publication of a letter does not constitute an endorsement of the views expressed. The only purpose of the Letters to the Editor column is to provide a forum for the expression of the readers" views. Our e-mail address is mmathew@isba.org   https://www.isba.org/IBJ/oct001/p554.htm
6/25/2009

Bar Journal

Letters to the Editor

Laurels for a laureate

Editor:

For several years I have been fortunate to know Warren Lupel, the laureate of the month of the Academy of Illinois Lawyers, and consider him a friend. Tom Johnson's moving portrait in the August issue, in the short space available, shows that it does more honor to the Academy to have Warren as a Laureate than vice versa. I am reminded that it is "far beyond our poor powers to add or detract" to his lifetime of service.

While it is certainly possible, as space permits, to add many additional features to Tom's tribute (but not enhance his eloquence), such as Warren's service with the Illinois Bar Foundation to name just one, the best way I can think to phrase it is that Warren Lupel makes me proud to be a lawyer.

— Phillip B. Lenzini
East Peoria, IL

Readers of the Journal are invited to submit short letters, preferably not exceeding 500 words, expressing their opinions, or giving information, as to any matter appearing in the Journal or otherwise. The editor reserves the right to select the communications or excerpts therefrom to publish and to edit for grammar and style. The publication of a letter does not constitute an endorsement of the views expressed. The only purpose of the Letters to the Editor column is to provide a forum for the expression of the readers' views. Our e-mail address is mmathew@isba.org.

July 14, 2009

Warren Lupel

Lupel Weininger LLP

30 North LaSalle Street

Suite 3520

Chicago, IL 60602

Re: Our appreciation

Dear Warren,

Meg and I cannot thank you enough for the outstanding work that you provided to Caroline You clearly dropped what you were otherwise doing, and on extremely short notice did what we believe no one else could have or would have done.

We also want to thank you for the extremely generous discount that you provided to us on our bill. It is greatly appreciated. We know that your and your colleagues' time is valuable and we thank you all.

If there is ever anything Meg or I can do for you or your family please do not hesitate to ask.

Gratefully.

We hope that this latest hurdle can be overcome.

July 14, 2009

Warren Lupel
Lupel Weininger LLP
30 North LaSalle Street
Suite 3520
Chicago, IL 60602

Re: Our appreciation

Dear Warren,

Meg and I cannot thank you enough for the outstanding work that you provided to Caroline.
You clearly dropped what you were otherwise doing, and on extremely short notice did what we
believe no one else could have or would have done.

We also want to thank you for the extremely generous discount that you provided to us on our
bill. It is greatly appreciated. We know that your and your colleagues' time is valuable and we
thank you all.

If there is ever anything Meg or I can do for you or your family please do not hesitate to ask.

Gratefully,

[signature]

We hope that this latest hurdle can be overcome.

JUSTICE ANN JORGENSEN

APPELLATE COURT 2nd DISTRICT

THANK YOU

We WON

We WON the Republican Primary

We WON every county

We Won with 153,996 votes

We WON with 66.7% of the vote

Every one of our supporters owns a piece of this win. Elections are not won from the top down-they are won from the bottom up. Everyone contributed-A Petition, A Contribution A sign in your yard, A friend-to-friend card, An introduction, an invitation to an event, A chance to speak to a group or organization A contact through a web connection, A Facebook friend or fan or, the immeasurable impact of email messages. Dem Warm, I can not think

Rich and I would not be here

without the support of each of you

Thank you for everything you have done for me Thank you for your confidence in me, and Thank you for your friendship

You wough for Your support.

To have the support of some one. I love Known & visputed for mimp

yours. mehms a grant dint Thank you Paid for by Citiem for Justice Ann Bjorgensen

JUSTICE ANN JORGENSEN
APPELLATE COURT 2nd DISTRICT

THANK YOU

We WON
We WON the Republican Primary
We WON every county
We Won with 153,996 votes
We WON with 66.7% of the vote

Every one of our supporters owns a piece of this win.
Elections are not won from the top down –they are won from the bottom up.
Everyone contributed-A Petition, A Contribution
A sign in your yard, A friend-to-friend card,
An introduction, an invitation to an event,
A chance to speak to a group or organization
A contact through a web connection,
A Facebook friend or fan or, the immeasurable impact of email messages.

Rich and I would not be here
without the support of each of you

Thank you for everything you have done for me
Thank you for your confidence in me, and
Thank you for your friendship.

Paid for by Citizens for Justice Ann B. Jorgensen.

LAW OFFICES

DAVIS FRIEDMAN ZAVETT KANE MACRAE MARCUS RUBENS

February 6, 2001

Warren Lupel, Esq.

Jonathan D. Sherman, Esq.

Katz, Randall, Weinberg & Richmond

333 W. Wacker Drive

Suite 1800

Chicago, IL 60606

RE: GERSON

Dear Warren and Jon:

I got the good word from Jon that the Illinois Supreme Court had denied the Gerson Petition for Leave to Appeal. I never doubted the outcome, but it is always good to have it in writing.

I want to repeat again that it was a pure joy to work with the two of you. My confidence never flagged because it was bred by being in the company of two very fine lawyers. I actually looked forward to our collaborations each step of the way. I always thought that the other side was over-matched. The entire saga was a pleasure, except, if I had had my druthers, I might have picked another defendant.

All the best from a devoted fan.

Sincerely yours

Muller

Muller Davis

MD/sv cc:

Melissa Kaplan, ISBA Mutual Insurance

MARQUETTE BUILDING SUITE 1000

TELEPHONE SO FACSIMILE S

99

BENJAMIN B. DAVIS (1910 - 1977)
WILLIAM C. BOYDEN (1946 - 1965)

LAW OFFICES

DAVIS · FRIEDMAN · ZAVETT
KANE · MACRAE · MARCUS · RUBENS

MULLER DAVIS, P.C.
ERROL ZAVETT
LARRY R. KANE, P.C.
RODERICK K. MACRAE
DORENE MARCUS, P.C.
JAMES T. RUBENS
JOSHUA J. FRIEDMAN

MURIEL KUHN
JODY MEYER YAZICI
SUSAN M. LAMPERT
DORIS S. McMORROW
DANIEL DONOHUE
DAVID G. AINLEY
BETH I. SCHWARZ

February 6, 2001

JAMES T. FRIEDMAN, OF COUNSEL

Warren Lupel, Esq.
Jonathan D. Sherman, Esq.
Katz, Randall, Weinberg & Richmond
333 W. Wacker Drive
Suite 1800
Chicago, IL 60606

RE: GERSON

Dear Warren and Jon:

I got the good word from Jon that the Illinois Supreme Court had denied the Gerson Petition for Leave to Appeal. I never doubted the outcome, but it is always good to have it in writing.

I want to repeat again that it was a pure joy to work with the two of you. My confidence never flagged because it was bred by being in the company of two very fine lawyers. I actually looked forward to our collaborations each step of the way. I always thought that the other side was over-matched. The entire saga was a pleasure, except, if I had had my druthers, I might have picked another defendant.

All the best from a devoted fan.

Sincerely yours,

Muller Davis

MD/sv
cc: Melissa Kaplan, ISBA Mutual Insurance

MARQUETTE BUILDING, SUITE 1600
140 SOUTH DEARBORN STREET, CHICAGO, ILLINOIS 60603
TELEPHONE 312·782·9220 FACSIMILE 312·782·9461

Rosen Law Firm

International Railroad Union

Approved Attorneys

1516 Vandalia Collinsville, no 62234

Telephone (618) 344-7540

Fax No. (618) 344-7567

January 14, 2000

Rick Rosen Principal

Dwight Hardin

PELA Consultant

Terence E. Flynn

William D. O'Donoghue

Of C

Donald F. Eddy of C

Warren Lupel, Esq.

Katz, Randall & Weinberg

333 West Wacker Dr., Ste. 1800

Chicago, IL 60606

Dear Warren,

Congratulations on being voted by your peers as a shining example of what's good about the legal profession. Not only are you a lawyer's lawyer and a man's man, but you are a "mensch" extraordinaire. Best regards to you and your family and I hope I don't "have" to see you soon.

Sincerely,

Rick Rosen

Chicago Office Suite 3100, 20 N. Clark Street, Chings, Illinois 6060

Rosen Law Firm
International Railroad Union Approved Attorneys

Rick Rosen
Principal

Dwight Hardin
FELA Consultant

1516 Vandalia
Collinsville, Illinois 62234
Telephone (618) 344-7540
Fax No. (618) 344-7567

Terence E. Flynn
Of Counsel

William D. O'Donaghue
Of Counsel

Donald F. Eddy
Of Counsel

January 14, 2000

Warren Lupel, Esq.
Katz, Randall & Weinberg
333 West Wacker Dr., Ste. 1800
Chicago, IL 60606

Dear Warren,

Congratulations on being voted by your peers as a shining example of what's good about the legal profession. Not only are you a lawyer's lawyer and a man's man, but you are a "mensch" extraordinaire. Best regards to you and your family and I hope I don't "have" to see you soon.

Sincerely,

Rick Rosen

RR/vkd

LAW OFFICES

HENRY T. SANDERS

Suite 2220

230 WEST MONROE STREET

CHICAGO, ILLINOIS 60606

February 7, 1999

Warren Lupel, Esq.

Katz, Randall & Weinberg

333 West Wacker Drive

Suite 1800

Chicago, IL 60606

Re: Henry T. Sandere

Commission No.

96 CH 633

Dear Warren,

Now that the time for appeal has run, I take this opportunity to thank you from the bottom of my heart for having represented me in this trying ordeal. You championed my cause when I was despa- rate. You performed in an outstanding manner. The "proof of the pudding ie in the eating: you won. I am forever in your debt. prove worthy of your performance. Believe me. I will endeavor to sincerely. HTS/xmp encl Henry T. Sanders

LAW OFFICES

HENRY T. SANDERS
Suite 2220
230 WEST MONROE STREET

CHICAGO, ILLINOIS 60606

—

(312) 782-6315

February 7, 1999

Warren Lupel, Esq.
Katz, Randall & Weinberg
333 West Wacker Drive
Suite 1800
Chicago, IL 60606

Re: Henry T. Sanders
Commission No.
96 CH 633

Dear Warren,

Now that the time for appeal has run, I take this opportunity to thank you from the bottom of my heart for having represented me in this trying ordeal. You championed my cause when I was desparate. You performed in an outstanding manner. The "proof of the pudding" is in the eating: you won.

I am forever in your debt. Believe me, I will endeavor to prove worthy of your performance.

Sincerely,

Henry T. Sanders

HTS/rmp
encl

104

Received at: 12,3/31/2005

State of Illinois

Circuit Court of Cook County

2001 Picha J. Daley Center

Chicago, in 60000

March 24, 2005

Dear Warren:

Congratulations! Mazel tov on the establishment of "The Warren Lopel" Fund.

Your good friend, Judge Abraham Lincoln Marovice, always spoke about the four crowns: Crown of Priesthood Crown of Nobility Crown of Torah And, the Fourth Crown, superior to them all and which you so distinguishably wear, the "Crown of a GoodName"

May you be blessed with all your good dreams being realized.

I am out of town on the 29 and, unfortunately, I cannot be present at your event. Enclosed please find a contribution to the Fund. JCB Enclosure Best regards,

State of Illinois
Circuit Court of Cook County

Gerald C. Bender
Judge

2801 Richard J. Daley Center
Chicago, Illinois 60602
(312) 603 3893
(312) 603-3892

March 24, 2005

Dear Warren:

Congratulations! Mazel tov on the establishment of "The Warren Lupel" Fund.

Your good friend, Judge Abraham Lincoln Marovitz, always spoke about the four crowns:

Crown of Priesthood
Crown of Nobility
Crown of Torah

And, the Fourth Crown, superior to them all and which you so distinguishably wear, the

"Crown of a Good Name."

May you be blessed with all your good dreams being realized.

I am out of town on the 29th and, unfortunately, I cannot be present at your event. Enclosed please find a contribution to the Fund.

Best regards,

Jerry Bender

JCB:rm
Enclosure

106

State of Illinois

Circuit Court of Cook County

Michael B. Hyman

November 29, 2010

50 West Washington Steer

Sue 2405

Richard J. Daley Center

Chicago, illinois 60602

(312) 603-3343

Dear Warren:

Mazel Tov on receiving the Award for Distinguished Service to Law & Society from IBF.

I am unable to attend to congratulate you in person, but wanted you to know that you have not only distinguished yourself in service to the profession and the community at large, but continuously, throughout your career, distinguished yourself by your example as the consummate caring lawyer devoted to serving causes that better the lives of others. Can any service be more distinguished?

May you continue to go from strength to strength, from success to success.

Very truly yours,

Judge Michael B. Hyman

State of Illinois
Circuit Court of Cook County
Chancery Division

Michael B. Hyman
Judge

50 West Washington Street
Suite 2405
Richard J. Daley Center
Chicago, Illinois 60602
(312) 603-3343

November 29, 2010

Dear Warren:

    Mazel Tov on receiving the Award for Distinguished Service to Law & Society from IBF.

    I am unable to attend to congratulate you in person, but wanted you to know that you have not only distinguished yourself in service to the profession and the community at large, but continuously, throughout your career, distinguished yourself by your example as the consummate caring lawyer devoted to serving causes that better the lives of others. Can any service be more distinguished?

    May you continue to go from strength to strength, from success to success.

Very truly yours,

Judge Michael B. Hyman

THE UNIVERSITY OF CHICAGO

THE LAW SCHOOL

III BAST 40TH STARRY

CHICAGO ILLINOIS 40437

May 24, 1985

Warren Lupel

2 North LaSalle Street

Chicago, IL 60602

Dear Warren:

Many thanks for your outstanding talk to my criminal law class on Wednesday. The students were enthusiastic about it, and so was I.

I commented to some students that your "lawyer's adventure" had the elements of a good Indiana Jones story: A mild-mannered college professor is plunged into the steaming jungle with earthquakes on the left and Nazi's on the right, but he handles it all with skill and aplomb. The students were impressed by your willingness to confess your "mistakes"; but the more I learn, the more it seems to me that you confronted an

extraordinary series of professional problems (ranging from structuring new administrative procedures to managing the media to researching the ancient law of coram nobis to attempting to reason with Born Again Christians)--and that, even with the benefit of hindsight, it is difficult to see how you could have done much better with them. So far as I can tell, you failed to give the slightest satisfaction to the snakes who were waiting for you to fall into the pit.

I'd be interested in seeing whatever briefs you file on both the recantation and phoney credentials issues. Please put me on your mailing list. And it can be of any help in reviewing the briefs or whatever, do let me know. I certainly owe you a favor.

Sincerely yours,

Albert W. Alschuler Professor of Law

THE UNIVERSITY OF CHICAGO
THE LAW SCHOOL
1111 EAST 60TH STREET
CHICAGO · ILLINOIS 60637

May 24, 1985

Warren Lupel
2 North LaSalle Street
Chicago, IL 60602

Dear Warren:

Many thanks for your outstanding talk to my criminal law class on Wednesday. The students were enthusiastic about it, and so was I.

I commented to some students that your "lawyer's adventure" had the elements of a good Indiana Jones story: A mild-mannered college professor is plunged into the steaming jungle with earthquakes on the left and Nazi's on the right, but he handles it all with skill and aplomb. The students were impressed by your willingness to confess your "mistakes"; but the more I learn, the more it seems to me that you confronted an extraordinary series of professional problems (ranging from structuring new administrative procedures to managing the media to researching the ancient law of coram nobis to attempting to reason with Born Again Christians)--and that, even with the benefit of hindsight, it is difficult to see how you could have done much better with them. So far as I can tell, you failed to give the slightest satisfaction to the snakes who were waiting for you to fall into the pit.

I'd be interested in seeing whatever briefs you file on both the recantation and phoney credentials issues. Please put me on your mailing list. And if I can be of any help in reviewing the briefs or whatever, do let me know. I certainly owe you a favor.

Sincerely yours,

Albert W. Alschuler
Professor of Law

110

NICHOLAS G. BYRON
CIRCUIT JUDGE
THIRD JUDICIAL CIRCUIT
STATE OF ILLINOIS

MADISON COUNTY COURTHOUSE

155 NORTH MAIN

EDWARDSVILLE, BLINOIS

PHONE-EXT4 FAX-475

June 17, 2004

Mr. Warren Lupel

Weinberg Richmond, LLP

333 West Wacker Drive, Ste. 1800

Chicago, IL 60606-1288

Dear Warren:

Words cannot describe my high esteem for you, and even in the short time I've come to know you I can truly say that I consider you a brother.

Thank you for your dedication and effort on my behalf.

Very truly yours.

Nicholas G. Byron

Circuit Judge

NICHOLAS G. BYRON
CIRCUIT JUDGE
THIRD JUDICIAL CIRCUIT
STATE OF ILLINOIS

MADISON COUNTY COURTHOUSE
155 NORTH MAIN
EDWARDSVILLE, ILLINOIS 62025
PHONE (618) 692-7040, EXT. 4885
FAX (618) 692-7473

June 17, 2004

Mr. Warren Lupel
Weinberg Richmond, LLP
333 West Wacker Drive, Ste. 1800
Chicago, IL 60606-1288

Dear Warren:

Words cannot describe my high esteem for you; and even in the short time I've come to know you I can truly say that I consider you a brother.

Thank you for your dedication and effort on my behalf.

Very truly yours,

Nicholas G. Byron
Circuit Judge

112

LAW OFFICE MANAGERS' ASSOCIATION OF CHICAGO

May 28, 1986

1966 OFFICERS & COMMITTEE CHAIRS

PRESENT

Kathleen M. Gyn

VICE PRESIDENT

SECRETARY

TREASURE

MEMBER AT LARGE

Schwar

K&Gay C 726-0845

PROGRAM and

CONTINUING EDUCATION Douglas R. Jackson

AUDIT

Raymond C

Mr. Warren Lupel, Esq. 30 North La Salle Street Chicago, Illinois 60603

Dear Warren

I cannot tell you how honored we were to have you at our podium. The people with whom I have spoken were unanimous in at least one sentiment: they all said they wished you could have stayed for another half hours that they weren't ready for it to end. For these people, Warren, that is the highest of high

praises.

with any kind of luck, the enclosed will express our gratitude. It isn't enough, we know. Thanks for a great afternoon. Very truly yours.

Bougia R.Jackson Program Chair

P.8.1 If your Administrator ever expresses an interest, I'm sure Marilyn Byrnes will be happy to provide her with all kinds of membership materials. We'd welcome her with open arms. DRJ

NEWSLETTER

HOTL

PUBLIC RELATIONS

Enclosure

236-2150

PAST PRESIDENT

Los A

LOMACA Leader in Developing Legal Administration Since 1952

LAW OFFICE MANAGERS' ASSOCIATION OF CHICAGO

**1986 OFFICERS &
COMMITTEE CHAIRS**

PRESIDENT
Kathleen M. Glynn
Shefsky, Saitlin
& Froelich, Ltd.
527-4000

VICE PRESIDENT
George W. Rupp
Bell, Boyd & Lloyd
372-1121

SECRETARY
Barbara S. Porter
Teller, Levit
& Silvertrust, P.C.
922-3030

TREASURER
Jo Ann Homan
Isham, Lincoln & Beale
558-7406

MEMBER AT LARGE
Colette M. Swiatkowski
Portes, Sharp, Herbst
& Kravets, Ltd.
372-1555

MEMBERSHIP
Marilyn J. Byrnes
Schwartz, Cooper,
Kolb & Gaynor, Chtd.
726-0845

**PROGRAM and
CONTINUING EDUCATION**
Douglas R. Jackson
McKenna, Storer, Rowe,
White & Farrug
558-8314

AUDIT
Raymond C. Heniff
Arvey, Hodes,
Costello & Burman
855-5095

NEWSLETTER
Patricia A. Schnepp
Cassiday, Schade & Gloor
641-3100

HOTLINE
Kenneth Watson, Jr.
Reuben & Proctor
558-5290

PUBLIC RELATIONS
Stephanie J. Storkel
Schumacher, Jones, Kelly,
Olson & Pusch
236-2150

PAST PRESIDENT
Lois Ann Satala
Baker & McKenzie
861-2905

May 28, 1986

Mr. Warren Lupel, Esq.
30 North La Salle Street
Chicago, Illinois 60603

Dear Warren:

I cannot tell you how honored we were to have
you at our podium. The people with whom I
have spoken were unanimous in at least one
sentiment: they all said they wished you
could have stayed for another half hour; that
they weren't ready for it to end. For these
people, Warren, that is the highest of high
praises.

With any kind of luck, the enclosed will
express our gratitude. It isn't enough,
we know. Thanks for a great afternoon.

Very truly yours,

Douglas R. Jackson
Program Chair

P.S.: If your Administrator ever expresses
an interest, I'm sure Marilyn Byrnes
will be happy to provide her with all
kinds of membership materials. We'd
welcome her with open arms. DRJ

Enclosure

LOMAC • A Leader in Developing Legal Administration Since 1952

BRESNAHAN, GARVEY, O'HALLORAN & COLEMAN

ATTORNEYS AND COUNSELORS AT LAM

RANDOLPH TOWER

188 WEST RANDOLPH STREET-SUITE 2415 CHICAGO, ILLINOIS 60601 (313) 880-0779

SUITE 204 (33

Dear Warren,

As our "Print Day" approaches I just wanted to thank you for letting big

article. It was of such the article is it will give me help you write our low reviews really exciting to be a small part Que and being involved with real honer. In addition, I think little edge in my career.

It was great clerking for you and I really didn't deserve the opportunity to write with

I just wanted to let you know that I'm very grateful.

Hope to see you soon!

Souy

BRESNAHAN, GARVEY, O'HALLORAN & COLEMAN
ATTORNEYS AND COUNSELORS AT LAW
RANDOLPH TOWER
168 WEST RANDOLPH STREET · SUITE 2413
CHICAGO, ILLINOIS 60601
(312) 580-0779

ARTHUR S. BRESNAHAN
KENNETH T. GARVEY
JOHN M. O'HALLORAN
JOHN M. COLEMAN
JUSTIN J. POWER
DOUGLAS MILLER

WHEATON OFFICE
104 E. ROOSEVELT ROAD
SUITE 204
WHEATON, ILLINOIS 60187
(312) 653-6333

Dear Warren,

As our "Print Day" approaches I just wanted to thank you for letting me help you write our law review article. It was really exciting to be a small part of such a big news case and being involved with the article is a real honor. In addition, I think it will give me a little edge in my career.

It was great clerking for you and I really didn't deserve the opportunity to write with you. I just wanted to let you know that I'm very grateful.

Hope to see you soon!

Doug

117

LAW OFFICES OF

MARTIN A. SMITH. LTD.

134 NORTH LASALLE STREET CHICAGO, ILLINOIS

76-44

Dean Warren,

My judgment won the respect to your ability was confirmal- ut instimet regarding you may gut. Compassion & consideration was correct.

Your friendship & cherish-

Thanks,

Beyz

LAW OFFICES OF
MARTIN A. SMITH, LTD.
SUITE 916
134 NORTH LA SALLE STREET
CHICAGO, ILLINOIS 60602
(312) 726-4204

Dear Warren —

My judgement with respect to your ability was confirmed — my gut instinct regarding your compassion & consideration was correct —

Your friendship I cherish —

Thanks,

Buzz

119

APPELLATE COURT OF ILLINOIS

RICHARD J. DALEY CENTER GOGOU

CHAMBERS OF

JUSTICE MICHEL A. COCCIA

June 8, 1990

012/790-5400

Mr. Warren Lupel

Lupel & Bunn

30 North La Salle Street, #2000

Chicago, IL 60602

My dear Warren:

Congratulations on being chosen by the Illinois State Bar Association to receive its prestigious Board of Governors Award! They like the rest of your friends in the Bar, recognize your exemplary service to the profession and to the Bar Association. and rejoice in your great achievement

You make us all very proud of your dedication to our profession and to the service of the people of Illinois. I am particularly proud of you and your individual contribution throughout these many years to the people and to the Bar, and you have all of my respect. I wish you the very best and I hope that I may have the privilege of seeing more of you during this year.

Warmest personal regards.

MAC der

MICHEL A. COCCIA

APPELLATE COURT OF ILLINOIS
RICHARD J. DALEY CENTER
60602

CHAMBERS OF
JUSTICE MICHEL A. COCCIA

312/793-5400

June 8, 1990

Mr. Warren Lupel
Lupel & Bunn
30 North La Salle Street, #2000
Chicago, IL 60602

My dear Warren:

Congratulations on being chosen by the Illinois State Bar Association to receive its prestigious Board of Governors Award! They, like the rest of your friends in the Bar, recognize your exemplary service to the profession and to the Bar Association, and we rejoice in your great achievement

You make us all very proud of your dedication to our profession and to the service of the people of Illinois. I am particularly proud of you and your individual contribution throughout these many years to the people and to the Bar, and you have all of my respect. I wish you the very best and I hope that I may have the privilege of seeing more of you during this year.

Warmest personal regards.

MICHEL A. COCCIA

MAC:dsr

DANCAVE DAN CAVETE PC.

ATTORNEYS AT LAW

June 18, 1993

Warren Lupel, Esq.

KATZ, RANDALL & WEINBERG

Suite 2300

200 N. LaSalle Street

Chicago, Illinois 60601-1097

Re: Robert Kaucher

Dear Mr. Lupel

I wanted to drop you a personal note thanking you for the excellent job that you did on behalf of my father. Not only was your lawyering of the highest quality, but you also provided excellent support and encouragement. This was one of the most difficult times my father has even been through in his life and he was greatly comforted by knowing that he had such excellent

representation.

Thank you again and best of luck to you and Pam.

JWK:din

Sincerely.

DAN CAVETT, P.C.

fi

By: Janes W. Kaucher

DAN CAVETT, P.C.
ATTORNEYS AT LAW
1860 EAST RIVER ROAD, SUITE 100
TUCSON, ARIZONA 85718-5870

DAN CAVETT
JAMES W. KAUCHER

TELEPHONE (602) 577-0400
FACSIMILE (602) 299-8860

June 18, 1993

Warren Lupel, Esq.
KATZ, RANDALL & WEINBERG
Suite 2300
200 N. LaSalle Street
Chicago, Illinois 60601-1097

    Re: Robert Kaucher

Dear Mr. Lupel:

    I wanted to drop you a personal note thanking you for the excellent job that you did on behalf of my father. Not only was your lawyering of the highest quality, but you also provided excellent support and encouragement. This was one of the most difficult times my father has even been through in his life and he was greatly comforted by knowing that he had such excellent representation.

    Thank you again and best of luck to you and Pam.

          Sincerely,

          DAN CAVETT, P.C.

          By: James W. Kaucher

JWK:dlm

John C. Dugan

ATTORNEY AT LAW

1000 SMOKIE BOULEVARD

WILMETTE, ILLINOIS GOOD

FAX O

March 23, 1995

PERSONAL

Mr. Warren Lupel

Katz, Randall & Wineberg

200 N. La Salle Street, Suite 2300 Chicago, IL 60601-1097

Re: KRW File

05624.00200

Dugan v. First Illinois Bank, et al.

Dear Warren:

At long last I am very pleased to be able to enclose my check payable to your firm in the amount of $2,000.00, this being in line with your letter to me of December 8, 1994. Quite frankly, I an somewhat embarrassed that it took so long to get this to you. on the other hand, I believe you can appreciate that this is a matter of personal pride with me and it does give me a great deal of satisfaction to have been able to carry my end of the bargain.

I do want to conclude this letter by stating that while I have been involved on many occasions with many attorneys, I have found no one as understanding and as sympathetic as yourself and at the same time extraordinarily competent.

Very truly yours,

co:vs

Dugan

John C. Dugan
ATTORNEY AT LAW

1000 SKOKIE BOULEVARD
WILMETTE, ILLINOIS 60091
———
(708) 256-7100
FAX (708) 256-0414

March 23, 1995

PERSONAL

Mr. Warren Lupel
Katz, Randall & Wineberg
200 N. La Salle Street, Suite 2300
Chicago, IL 60601-1097

Re: KRW File 05624.00200
     Dugan v. First Illinois Bank, et al.

Dear Warren:

At long last I am very pleased to be able to enclose my check payable to your firm in the amount of $2,000.00, this being in line with your letter to me of December 8, 1994. Quite frankly, I am somewhat embarrassed that it took so long to get this to you. On the other hand, I believe you can appreciate that this is a matter of personal pride with me and it does give me a great deal of satisfaction to have been able to carry my end of the bargain.

I do want to conclude this letter by stating that while I have been involved on many occasions with many attorneys, I have found no one as understanding and as sympathetic as yourself and at the same time extraordinarily competent.

Very truly yours,

John C. Dugan

JCD:ws

125

Sara R. Howard

Attorney at Law

3247 N. Elston Avenue

Chicago, Minois 60618

773/509-1818

Fax 509-1888

10-2-98

Dear Warren-

There aren't enough words to express my thanks for all

your effort, time and consideration these past several years! my gosh-who would Have you ever thought it would go so far. Please accept my! Years humble thanks for all you've done, and expecially for who you are. Thank you

Sincerely,

Sara Howard

Sara R. Howard
Attorney at Law

3247 N. Elston Avenue
Chicago, Illinois 60618

773/ 509-1818
fax 509-1888

10-2-98

Dear Warren –

There aren't enough words to express
my thanks for all your effort, time
and consideration these past several
years — years! My gosh – who would
have thought it would go so far.

Please accept my humble thanks
for all you've done, and especially
for who you are. Thank you.

Sincerely,

Sara Howard

Paul E. Elward

Lawyer

1532 West Chase Avenue

Chicago Illinois 60626.2126

Tel. & Fax 773.274-3648

September 27, 2000

Dean Warren,

Please accept Related congratulate

On being Misson a Caurants forthe Alading of Kimis Sawyers. It in and is an loude richly zerons by you.

Cordially hul

Paul F. Elward
Lawyer

1532 West Chase Avenue
Chicago, Illinois 60626-2126

Tel. & Fax
773.274.3648

September 27, 2000

Dear Warren,

Please accept belated congratulations on being chosen a laureate for the Academy of Illinois Lawyers. It was an honor richly earned by you.

Truly,

Paul

PECK, BLOOM, AUSTRIACO & MITCHELL, LLC

ATTORNEYS AT LAW

FOR WEST ADAMS STREET TRINIY

CHICAGO, ILLINGS GOROS TELEPHONE
131212010000 FACOMILE (312) 20-0003

T FLOOR

April 20, 2005

Warren Lupel, Esq. Weinberg & Richmond

333 W. Wacker, Suite 1800

Chicago, Illinois 60606-1288

Re:

Warren Lupel Fund

Dear Warren:

you.

You are incredible! Thank you for all the great work that you do and I am so proud of you!

I am sorry that I missed your reception but here's a little contribution for the fund named after

AAA m Enclosure

Sincerely,

POCK, PEDOM, AUSTRIACO & MITCHELL, LLC

Ayfora Abella-Austriaco

Great job, Warren!

PECK, BLOOM, AUSTRIACO & MITCHELL, LLC
ATTORNEYS AT LAW

KERRY H. PECK*
JENNIFER M. BLOOM

GAY J. ROSENG III
PETER E. CHUN AN
ALEXANDER BRATATSKY
MARISA M. ZUPAN A
JEANNE M. CUNNINGHAM
ANDREA AVENENTA

OF COUNSEL
AURORA ABELLA-AUSTRIACO
JEROME G. MILLER, RETIRED
W. REBECCA MITCHELL
JOSEPH PECK

*ALSO ADMITTED IN FLORIDA

105 WEST ADAMS STREET · THIRTY-FIRST FLOOR
(ENTER BUILDING AT 210 SOUTH CLARK STREET)
CHICAGO, ILLINOIS 60603
TELEPHONE (312) 201-0900
FACSIMILE (312) 201-0803
WWW.PECKBLOOM.COM

NORTHBROOK
801 NORTH SKOKIE BLVD
SUITE 1A, EARTH LAW BLDG
NORTHBROOK, IL 60062
(847) 509-1099

OFFICES IN FLORIDA

April 20, 2005

Warren Lupel, Esq.
Weinberg & Richmond
333 W. Wacker, Suite 1800
Chicago, Illinois 60606-1288

Re: *Warren Lupel Fund*

Dear Warren:

You are incredible! Thank you for all the great work that you do and I am so proud of you!

I am sorry that I missed your reception but here's a little contribution for the fund named after you.

Sincerely,

PECK, BLOOM, AUSTRIACO & MITCHELL, LLC

Aurora Abella-Austriaco

AAA:nm
Enclosure

Great job, Warren!

JAMERA MAN

LAW OFFICES OF

ANTHONY C. RACCUGLIA & ASSOCIATES

PERU, ILLINOIS 8135-4

FIRST FEDERAL SAVLONDO

December 9, 2002

Warren Lupel

Katz, Randall, Weinberg, & Richmond 333 W. Wacker Drive, Suite 1800 Chicago, IL 60606

PERSONAL AND CONFIDENTIAL

Dear Warren:

How wonderfully generous of you to take the time to participate with Mike Reagan to put my name before the committee for an appointment to the academy. I must tell you that no matter how great the honor is to have been selected, I was a winner long before I was told that I was selected given the fact that people like yourself wrote such glowing recommendations for my appointment.

I have the utmost respect for you as a human being and as a lawyer and the way you were able to take me and Cindy through the very difficult several years will never be forgotten. I know that you did go the extra mile for us and I know that you would hurt as much as I would when things were not going quite our way at the early stages of the proceeding.

That being said, it was obvious right from the beginning that you were my kind of guy. From the bad came the good. I truly believe that you and I will always have a friendship relationship and I will always feel a sense of joy when I read your name in the Law Bulletin or other bar publications when you become involved in another one of your projects to help the legal system, as well as the people involved.

Words cannot describe how I feel about your generosity in becoming involved in this project. I guess when that happens; the best to be said is a simple "thank you".

With very kindest personal regards,

Toy

LAW OFFICES OF

ANTHONY C. RACCUGLIA & ASSOCIATES

JAMES A. McPHEDRAN
LOUIS L. BERTRAND
ASSOCIATE COUNSEL

1200 MAPLE DRIVE
PERU, ILLINOIS 61354
TELEPHONE (815) 223-0230
FAX (815) 223 0293

OTTAWA OFFICE
SUITE 403
633 LASALLE STREET
FIRST FEDERAL SAVINGS & LOAN BLDG.
TEL (815) 434-2003

December 9, 2002

Warren Lupel
Katz, Randall, Weinberg, & Richmond
333 W. Wacker Drive, Suite 1800
Chicago, IL 60606

PERSONAL AND CONFIDENTIAL

Dear Warren:

How wonderfully generous of you to take the time to participate with Mike Reagan to put my name before the committee for an appointment to the academy. I must tell you that no matter how great the honor is to have been selected, I was a winner long before I was told that I was selected given the fact that people like yourself wrote such glowing recommendations for my appointment.

I have the utmost respect for you as a human being and as a lawyer and the way you were able to take me and Cindy through the very difficult several years will never be forgotten. I know that you did go the extra mile for us and I know that you would hurt as much as I would when things were not going quite our way at the early stages of the proceeding.

That being said, it was obvious right from the beginning that you were my kind of guy. From the bad came the good. I truly believe that you and I will always have a friendship relationship and I will always feel a sense of joy when I read your name in the Law Bulletin or other bar publications when you become involved in another one of your projects to help the legal system, as well as the people involved.

Words cannot describe how I feel about your generosity in becoming involved in this project. I guess when that happens; the best to be said is a simple "thank you".

With very kindest personal regards,

Tony

THE JOHN MARSHALL LAW SCHOOL" 315 South Plymouth Court
Chicago, Illinois 60004 www.mix.edu 1000

CENTENNIAL

PAULAH DEMAN

August 17, 1998

Mr. Warren Lupel

Katz, Randall & Weinberg

333 W. Wacker Drive, Suite 1800

Chicago, IL 60606

Dear Warren:

I wanted to drop you a note to say how wonderful the article about you in the ISBA News was. Obviously, the subject matter was not wonderful, but the fact you went over there and contributed your time and your skill was truly remarkable. Thank you for bringing to our attention the awful plight of Indian women and children. Your efforts will surely help.

Many of us think about the dire circumstances of others, but we do little about it.

Your action is an example for all of us, Warren.

Sincerely yours. Pane Paula Hadson Holderman

THE JOHN MARSHALL LAW SCHOOL®
315 South Plymouth Court   Chicago, Illinois 60604   www.jmls.edu

CENTENNIAL
1899-1999

Tel: 312.427.2737
Fax: 312.427.9974

PAULA H. HOLDERMAN
Assistant Director,
Center for Advocacy and Dispute Resolution
Acting Director,
Clinical Education Program
Direct: 312-987-2394
Fax: 312-427-0974
Inct. hholderm@jmls.edu

August 17, 1998

Mr. Warren Lupel
Katz, Randall & Weinberg
333 W. Wacker Drive, Suite 1800
Chicago, Il 60606

Dear Warren:

I wanted to drop you a note to say how wonderful the article about you in the ISBA News was. Obviously, the subject matter was not wonderful, but the fact you went over there and contributed your time and your skill was truly remarkable. Thank you for bringing to our attention the awful plight of Indian women and children. Your efforts will surely help.

Many of us think about the dire circumstances of others, but we do little about it. Your action is an example for all of us, Warren.

Sincerely yours,

Paula Hudson Holderman

HOUSE OF KLEEN

955 SO. ELMHURST ROAD

437-7141

Dear Warren;

10/1/15

When a man a4 takes the time to man (my son) a bury as you beautifully dis, It means that you are very special person.

We believe Ron may pull out big financial problems with

Thank you

Jebeir

Filmen

"Think Kleen"

☀ ⧽OUSE of ⧽LEEN

955 SO. ELMHURST ROAD
DES PLAINES, ILL. 60018
437-7141

10/9/75

Dear Warren;

When a man as busy as you are,
takes the time to council a young
man (my son) as beautifuly as you
did, I means that you are a
very special person.

We believe Ron may pull out of
his finencial problems with your help.

Thank you

Julius Gilman

━━━━━━━━━━━━━ *"Think Kleen"* ━━━━━━━━━━━━━

138

LAW OFFICES

DAVIS FRIEDMAN ZAVETT KANE MACRAE

August 8, 2000

LARRY KANE RODERICK MACAR

Warren Lupel, Esq.

Katz, Randall, Weinberg & Richmond

333 West Wacker Drive

Suite 1800

Chicago, Illinois 60606

Dear Warren:

Congratulations on being one of the laureates of the Academy of Illinois Lawyers. I read with great pleasure the article about you in the August Illinois Ilar Journal. I have always admired your work on behalf of those who could not afford you, and your honor as a laureate was obviously greatly deserved. We can all use you as a model for the delivery of legal services to the indigent, a cause in which I believe.

All the best

Sincerely yours

Muller Davis

MD/Wr

BENJAMIN B. DAVIS (1940 - 1971)
WILLIAM C. BOYDEN (1940 - 1963)

LAW OFFICES

DAVIS·FRIEDMAN
ZAVETT·KANE·MACRAE

MULLER DAVIS, P.C.
ERROL ZAVETT
LARRY B. KANE, P.C.
RODERICK E. MALMAS
JAMES L. RUBENS
DORENE MARCUS, P.C.
MURIEL KIMS
JOSHUA F. FRIEDMAN
JODY MEYER YAZICI
SUSAN M. LAMPERT
DORIS S. McMORROW
DANIEL DONOHUE
DAVID C. AINLEY

JAMES T. FRIEDMAN, OF COUNSEL

August 8, 2000

Warren Lupel, Esq.
Katz, Randall, Weinberg & Richmond
333 West Wacker Drive
Suite 1800
Chicago, Illinois 60606

Dear Warren:

Congratulations on being one of the laureates of the Academy of Illinois Lawyers. I read with great pleasure the article about you in the August Illinois Bar Journal. I have always admired your work on behalf of those who could not afford you, and your honor as a laureate was obviously greatly deserved. We can all use you as a model for the delivery of legal services to the indigent, a cause in which I believe.

All the best.

Sincerely yours,

Muller Davis

MD/wr

MARQUETTE BUILDING SUITE 1600
140 SOUTH DEARBORN STREET CHICAGO ILLINOIS 60603
TELEPHONE 312·782·2220 FACSIMILE 312·782·0464

Mare J. Zimring, D.D.S.

PERIODONTICS EXCLUSIVELY FORTY-SIX EAST GAK STREET CHICAGO, ILLINOIS BO

Jonny

As a "The gust

and wise man once said унав Quite

from your Cassatility

a truly that alone has

Please accept This with most sincere and ту

I love Men P.S.

Interen the then of as an oberones sincriity and alloway. You han piran

prant more to me then I can before hanstylt apprssination.

A gust and wise man once also said "I want to hear nothing. Enjoy !! more about it

PERIODONTICS EXCLUSIVELY
FORTY-SIX EAST OAK STREET
CHICAGO, ILLINOIS 60611
312 649-0560

Marc J. Zimring, D.D.S.

Jonny

As a great and wise man once said —
"This is just between the three of us."

Aside from your obvious sincerity and
capability as an attorney, you have proven
yourself a true friend — that alone has
meant more to me than I can express.
Please accept this with my most sincere and
heartfelt appreciation.

I love you

 - Alan

P.S. A great and wise man once also said
"I want to hear nothing more about it."

Enjoy !!

142

Law Offices

Quinn, Johnston, Henderson & Pretorius

Chartered

September 23, 2004

Michael Hende Marvel

Bray W. Dunham

Onguty A. Cer

Jam And David Cl

Michal H

P

Michel A. Krah

Jo T. Wh

Alison N. Bell Adam P. Cha

Ms. Susan Pierson

Illinois Bar Foundation c/o Illinois State Bar Assn. 424 S. Second Street Springfield, IL 61701-1704

Dear Susan:

I enclose a check in the amount of $100 for the Warren Lupel Fund. Warren is one of the finest attorneys and persons I have had the pleasure to know. The seed money from his grateful clients speaks volumes about both his abilities and personality.

Good luck with the fundraiser.

Very truly yours,

Quinn, Johnston, Hendergon & Pretorius

By:

Brick

R. Michael Henderson

Lowell R. McCl

Golden A. McCl

Jorg A. Link

Richard Qui

(217) 753-433

Fax: (217) 755-180

RMH/rea Encl.

cc: Warren Lupel

Law Offices
Quinn, Johnston, Henderson & Pretorius
Chartered

Telephone: (309) 674-1133   227 N.E. Jefferson Street   email: quinnlaw@qjhp.com
Fax: (309) 674-6503   Peoria, Illinois 61602   Website: http://www.qjhp.com

R. Michael Henderson
Murvel Pretorius, Jr.
Bradley W. Dunham
Robert H. Jennetten
Gregory A. Cerulo
Paul P. Gilfillan
Laurie M. Judd
Stanley L. Morris
James A. Borland
David R. Collins
John F. Kamin
Michael J. Holt
Matthew B. Smith
Peter R. Jennetten
Michael A. Kraft
Matthew J. Maddox
Jonathan A. Stump
Laura A. Petersen
Kevin M. Miller

Jo T. Wetherill
John D. Moses
John A. Walters
Allison N. Bell
Adam P. Chaddock
Melinda M. Rowe
Claire E. Craig

of Counsel
W. Thomas Johnston

Lowell R. McConnell
(1911-1931)
Golden A. McConnell
(1911-1974)
Joseph A. Leinikoehler
(1931-1974)
Thomas B. Kennedy, Sr.
(1912-1988)
William C. Nicol
(1911-1996)
John C. Newell, Jr.
(1915-1996)
Richard E. Quinn
(1926-2000)

Springfield Office
205 South Fifth Street
Suite 900
Springfield, IL 62701
Telephone: (217) 753-1133
Fax: (217) 753-1180

September 23, 2004

Ms. Susan Pierson
Illinois Bar Foundation
c/o Illinois State Bar Assn.
424 S. Second Street
Springfield, IL 61701-1704

Dear Susan:

I enclose a check in the amount of $100 for the Warren Lupel Fund. Warren is one of the finest attorneys and persons I have had the pleasure to know. The seed money from his grateful clients speaks volumes about both his abilities and personality.

Good luck with the fundraiser.

Very truly yours,

Quinn, Johnston, Henderson & Pretorius

By: R. Michael Henderson

RMH/rea
Encl.
cc: Warren Lupel

LOUISE OLIVERO

DOUGLAS B. OLIVERO** DAVID W.OLIVERO

LARRY MILLER

Mr. Warren Lupel

Attorney at Law

LAW OFFICES OF

Lous E. OVER & ASSOCIATES

1615 FOURTH STREET PERU, ILLINOIS 4354

January 10, 2005

AREA CODE TELEPHONE 224200 FAX 224-JOT

333 West Wacker Drive, Suite 1800

Chicago, Illinois 60606-1288

Dear Warren:

Enclosed is my business account check in the sum of $2,729.50 in payment of Invoice No. 113743, a copy of which is also enclosed.

I would like to take this opportunity to thank you all your help during this difficult time. I was so fortunate to find a lawyer like yourself who was willing to stand up for the rights of a colleague. You also deserve the gratitude of the entire legal profession for your tireless efforts in exonerating innocent persons from the shadow of suspicion for life.

Thank you again, and best wishes for a Happy, Healthy and Prosperous New Year.

LEO as Enc. (2)

Very truly yours,

LOUIS E. OLIVERO & ASSOCIATES

By Louis E. Olivero

LAW OFFICES OF
Louis E. Olivero & Associates
1615 FOURTH STREET
PERU, ILLINOIS 61354

LOUIS E. OLIVERO *

DOUGLAS B. OLIVERO **
DAVID W. OLIVERO
LARRY E. SITTLER

AREA CODE 815
TELEPHONE 224-2400
FAX 223-3075

January 10, 2005

Mr. Warren Lupel
Attorney at Law
333 West Wacker Drive, Suite 1800
Chicago, Illinois 60606-1288

Dear Warren:

Enclosed is my business account check in the sum of $2,729.50 in payment of Invoice No. 113743, a copy of which is also enclosed.

I would like to take this opportunity to thank you all your help during this difficult time. I was so fortunate to find a lawyer like yourself who was willing to stand up for the rights of a colleague. You also deserve the gratitude of the entire legal profession for your tireless efforts in exonerating innocent persons from the shadow of suspicion for life.

Thank you again, and best wishes for a Happy, Healthy and Prosperous New Year.

Very truly yours,

LOUIS E. OLIVERO & ASSOCIATES

By Louis E. Olivero

LEO:as
Enc. (2)

147

315 SOUTH PLYMOUTH COURT

CHICAGO, ILLINOIS 40404

312/427-3737

The John Marshall Law School

March 13,1987

Warren Lupel

Solomon Rosenfeld Elliott & stiefel Ltd

30 N. Lasalle St.

Chicago, Illinois 60601

Dear Mr. Lupel.

On behalf of The John Marshall Law School Alumni Association. it. is our sincere pleasure to inform you that you have been selected to receive the 1987 Distinguished Service Award, the highest accolade conferred on alumni of the Law School. Your record of professional excellence and service to the community commend you most highly as a recepient.

The 1987 Distinguished Service Awards will be presented at a luncheon at the Palmer House on Thursday, May 14.

Tickets will be provided for you and a guest. We will be happy to send invitations to your personal guest list if you will send us names of friends, family, and business associates who want to be there as you are honored by your fellow John Marshall Alumni and other members of Chicago's legal community.

If you have any questions regarding this event, please call Ruth Ganchiff Director of Development and Alumni Programs at 987-1412. Also, please forward to her a black and white photo, any additional biographical materials that might be helpful in preparing your biography for the program, and your personal invitation list.

We look forward to being with you on May 14.

Sincerely.

Crear Gottman

Robert Guttman President

Alumni Assoc.

سمت سزا

Timothy Evans General Luncheon Chairman

Thomas F. Peterson

Thomas F. Peterson Awards Chairman

The John Marshall Law School does not discriminate in admissions, services, or employment on the basis of sex, race

315 SOUTH PLYMOUTH COURT • CHICAGO, ILLINOIS 60604   312/427.2737

The John Marshall Law School

March 13, 1987

Warren Lupel
Solomon Rosenfeld Elliott & Stiefel Ltd
30 N. LaSalle St.
Chicago, Illinois 60601

Dear Mr. Lupel,

On behalf of The John Marshall Law School Alumni Association, it
is our sincere pleasure to inform you that you have been selected
to receive the 1987 Distinguished Service Award, the highest
accolade conferred on alumni of the Law School.   Your record of
professional excellence and service to the community commend you
most highly as a recepient.

The 1987 Distinguished Service Awards will be presented at a
luncheon at the Palmer House on Thursday, May 14.

Tickets will be provided for you and a guest. We will be happy
to send invitations to your personal guest list if you will send
us names of friends, family, and business associates who want to
be there as you are honored by your fellow John Marshall Alumni
and other members of Chicago's legal community.

If you have any questions regarding this event, please call Ruth
Ganchiff, Director of Development and Alumni Programs at 987-
1412.   Also, please forward to her a black and white photo, any
additional biographical materials that might be helpful in
preparing your biography for the program, and your personal
invitation list.

We look forward to being with you on May 14.

Sincerely,

Robert Guttman
President
Alumni Assoc.

Timothy Evans
General Luncheon
Chairman

Thomas F. Peterson
Awards Chairman

LAW OFFICES

ROBERT P. CUMMINS. P. C.

1 SOUTH LA BALLE STREET CHICAGO, ILLINOIS 60003

Warren Lupel

Lupel and Amari

Two North LaSalle Street Suite 1906

Chicago, Illinois 60602

December 6, 1984

Dear Warren:

The following is an excerpt from the trial proceedings before Judge Getzendanner on Friday, the 30th of November:

THE COURTI But I am not talking about that early on. Mr. Lupel litigated the contempt hearing. Mr. Lupel had access to these documents.

abilities.

I had a great deal of respect for Mr. Lupel's He is one of the best lawyers I have seen try a

case in my courtroom.

My best regards.

RPC/m

Stacerely.

Robert P. Cummins

suitable for freaming

LAW OFFICES

ROBERT P. CUMMINS, P. C.
19 SOUTH LASALLE STREET
CHICAGO, ILLINOIS 60603
(312) 702-1551

December 6, 1984

Warren Lupel
Lupel and Amari
Two North LaSalle Street
Suite 1906
Chicago, Illinois 60602

Dear Warren:

The following is an excerpt from the trial proceedings before Judge Getzendanner on Friday, the 30th of November:

THE COURT: But I am not talking about that early on. Mr. Lupel litigated the contempt hearing. Mr. Lupel had access to these documents.

I had a great deal of respect for Mr. Lupel's abilities. He is one of the best lawyers I have seen try a case in my courtroom.

My best regards.

Sincerely,

Robert P. Cummins

RPC/mul

This letter is suitable for framing!

152

THE UNIVERSITY OF CHICAGO

THE LAW SCHOOL

1111 BAST 40TH STREET CHICAGO ILLINOIS 60637

May 9, 1985

Warren Lupel, Esq.

2 North La Salle

Chicago, Illinois 60602

Dear Mr. Lupel

I enclose a copy of a letter that I sent today to the editor of the Chicago Sun-Times.

Although the Sun-Times story is the worst of the bunch, it is not the only one that has said or implied that I have been critical of your handling of the Dotson case. For example, a reporter named Mara Tapp called me last weekend to talk about a story and began by reading another story that she had printed somewhere. (I still haven't seen it.) The story said something about how I had initially been critical of Marren Lupel but had changed my mind. Although Ms. Tapp had obviously made her error unintentionally (or she wouldn't have been so quick to read the story to me), I hit the ceiling. 1 have never said anything critical of your work to anyone.

In fact, although I am obviously in no position to pass Judgment, everything that I know suggests that your handling of the Dotson case has been admirable (and I have said that to reporters, including the Sun-Times creep). Your motion to vacate the judgment was plainly the only legally available remedy under 111inois law, and the "leaders" of the defense bar who would have slammed into court on a PC petition without doing the necessary book work would have been courting disaster. You have had some delicate lines to walk in relations with the press and the like, and so far as I can tell, you've done an outstanding job of it. I regret that some reporters have made my position seem the opposite of the one that I hold in fact.

153

June On a different matter, my first-year criminal law class at the University of Chicago will meet on Tuesdays, Wednesdays and Thursdays at 11:15 a.m. until Once the air has cleared, you will probably want to head for a beach somewhere. But if you thought it appropriate to share your adventures with the students and if you had the time, we'd enjoy viating with you. Please give me a call at 962-3586 (office) or 493-2706 (home) if you might be persuaded to come to the South Side and reminisce about your recent, distinctive professional experience. I promise: There will be no goddamn reporterat

AWAll

Sincerely yours.

Albert W. Alschuler Professor of Law

May 9, 1985

Warren Lupel, Esq.
2 North La Salle
Chicago, Illinois 60602

Dear Mr. Lupel:

I enclose a copy of a letter that I sent today to the editor of the
Chicago Sun-Times.

Although the Sun-Times story is the worst of the bunch, it is not the
only one that has said or implied that I have been critical of your handling
of the Dotson case. For example, a reporter named Mara Tapp called me last
weekend to talk about a story and began by reading another story that she had
printed somewhere. (I still haven't seen it.) The story said something about
how I had initially been critical of Warren Lupel but had changed my mind.
Although Ms. Tapp had obviously made her error unintentionally (or she
wouldn't have been so quick to read the story to me), I hit the ceiling. I
have never said anything critical of your work to anyone.

In fact, although I am obviously in no position to pass judgment,
everything that I know suggests that your handling of the Dotson case has been
admirable (and I have said that to reporters, including the Sun-Times
creep). Your motion to vacate the judgment was plainly the only legally
available remedy under Illinois law, and the "leaders" of the defense bar who
would have slammed into court on a PC petition without doing the necessary
book work would have been courting disaster. You have had some delicate lines
to walk in relations with the press and the like, and so far as I can tell,
you've done an outstanding job of it. I regret that some reporters have made
my position seem the opposite of the one that I hold in fact.

On a different matter, my first-year criminal law class at the University
of Chicago will meet on Tuesdays, Wednesdays and Thursdays at 11:15 a.m. until
June 4. Once the air has cleared, you will probably want to head for a beach
somewhere. But if you thought it appropriate to share your adventures with
the students and if you had the time, we'd enjoy visting with you. Please
give me a call at 962-3586 (office) or 493-2706 (home) if you might be
persuaded to come to the South Side and reminisce about your recent,
distinctive professional experience. I promise: There will be no goddamn
reporters!

Sincerely yours,

Albert W. Alschuler
Professor of Law

AWA:sll

155

THE UNIVERSITY OF CHICAGO

THE LAW SCHOOL

1111 EAST 60TH STREET CHICAGO ILLINOIS 40437

May 9, 1985

Editor

Chicago Sun-Times 401 North Wabash

Chicago, Illinois 60611

Dear Editori

Throughout a lengthy interview yesterday, a Sun Times reporter, Fran Spielman, pressed me to criticize the work of Gary Dotson's attorney, Warren Lupel. I declined to do so. Undaunted by her failure to obtain the comment that she sought, Ms. Spielman appears to have made one up.

During our conversation, I said that if Lupel had failed to interview his witnesses and learn what they would say prior to the hearing, before Judge Samuels, that failure would qualify as a legitimate basis for criticism. I added, however, that I had no reason to believe that Lupel had failed in this respect. Indeed, I told the reporter that I had met Lupel when we appeared together on a TV program. In a brief moment of "lawyers' talk" before the program went on the air, I had asked whether Lupel had been surprised by the inconsistency in the alibi testimony presented at the hearing. Lupel replied that he had not been surprised and said that he had initially advised his client not to testify in order to avoid this inconsistency. Lupel had relented only because Dotson had wanted to testify and because Lupel had concluded, perhaps erroneously, that a discrepancy in the evidence concerning a fifteen-minute period seven years ago would not be particularly damaging.

In this morning's paper, this conversation la reported as follows: The preparation of witnesses is an essential ingredient, and for that he [Lupel] should be criticized," University of Chicago Law Professor Albert W. Alschuler said."

Congratulations! The Chicago Sun Times has again won the J. R. Eving Award for Ethics in Journalist

Sincerely yours,

Albert W. Alschuler Professor of Law

AWAI811

ce: Warren Lupel

THE UNIVERSITY OF CHICAGO

THE LAW SCHOOL

1111 EAST 60TH STREET

CHICAGO · ILLINOIS 60637

May 9, 1985

Editor
Chicago Sun-Times
401 North Wabash
Chicago, Illinois 60611

Dear Editor:

　　Throughout a lengthy interview yesterday, a Sun Times reporter, Fran Spielman, pressed me to criticize the work of Gary Dotson's attorney, Warren Lupel. I declined to do so. Undaunted by her failure to obtain the comment that she sought, Ms. Spielman appears to have made one up.

　　During our conversation, I said that if Lupel had failed to interview his witnesses and learn what they would say prior to the hearing before Judge Samuels, that failure would qualify as a legitimate basis for criticism. I added, however, that I had no reason to believe that Lupel had failed in this respect. Indeed, I told the reporter that I had met Lupel when we appeared together on a TV program. In a brief moment of "lawyers' talk" before the program went on the air, I had asked whether Lupel had been surprised by the inconsistency in the alibi testimony presented at the hearing. Lupel replied that he had not been surprised and said that he had initially advised his client not to testify in order to avoid this inconsistency. Lupel had relented only because Dotson had wanted to testify and because Lupel had concluded, perhaps erroneously, that a discrepancy in the evidence concerning a fifteen-minute period seven years ago would not be particularly damaging.

　　In this morning's paper, this conversation is reported as follows: "'The preparation of witnesses is an essential ingredient, and for that he [Lupel] should be criticized,' University of Chicago Law Professor Albert W. Alschuler said."

　　Congratulations! The Chicago Sun Times has again won the J. R. Ewing Award for Ethics in Journalism!

　　　　　　　　　　　　Sincerely yours,

　　　　　　　　　　　　Albert W. Alschuler
　　　　　　　　　　　　Professor of Law

AWA:sll

cc: Warren Lupel

Hona Bobak

242 8. Cd Canyon #B. Orange, CA 92869 (714) 638-4212

December, 2008

Dear.

Mr. Warren Lupel

I appreciate your care and dedication you have given me throughout the years. I am especially grateful for Attorneys like yourself.

In this special Holiday Season, I give to you and your family the best of wishes. May God bless you and your family.

Sincerely.

Ilona

Ilona Bobak

Ilona Bobak

242 S. Crawford Canyon #8, Orange, CA 92869
(714) 538-4212

December, 2008

Dear,
   Mr. Warren Lupel

I appreciate your care and dedication you have given me throughout the years. I am especially grateful for Attorneys like yourself.

In this special Holiday Season, I give to you and your family the best of wishes. May God bless you and your family.

Sincerely,

Ilona Bobak

Franks Gerkin McKenna, P.C.

July 20, 2004

Mr. Warren Lupel

Katz, Randall, Weinberg & Richmond

333 Wacker Drive, Ste 1800

Chicago, Illinois 60606-1226

Dear Karren:

Thank you so much for your tremendous assistance in my recons troubles. Martin Luther King once said that he didn't remember the words of his enemies but did remember the silence of his friends.

I very much appreciate you being there for me and so vocal.

With warm Regards,,

FRANS ERKIN & KEN, P.C.

Jack Franks JDF/p

1955 Fase GeHighway

PO Box

Marengs, 2000

Franks Gerkin McKenna, P.C.
Lawyers

July 20, 2004

Mr. Warren Lupel
Katz, Randall, Weinberg & Richmond
333 W Wacker Drive, Ste 1800
Chicago, Illinois 60606-1226

Dear Warren:

Thank you so much for your tremendous assistance in my recent troubles. Martin Luther King once said that he didn't remember the words of his enemies but did remember the silence of his friends.

I very much appreciate you being there for me and so vocal.

With Warm Regards,

FRANKS, GERKIN & McKENNA, P.C.

Jack D. Franks
JDF/pk

2555 Fox Grant Highway
PO Box 5
Marengo, Illinois 60152-0005
Tel 815 923 2107
Email: FranLaw@aol.net
Fax 815 923 2114

162

May 22, 1989

Mr. Warren G. Lupel

Lupel & Bunn

30 North La Salle Street, #2000 Chicago, IL 60602

Dear Warren:

Congratulations to you for your out- standing effort and success in running for the Assembly of the Illinois State Bar Association.

I am simply thrilled with the fact that you are interested in the management of our Illinois State Bar Association."

I look forward to watching your illus trious career with the Bar and only hope that you will continue on with the giving of more definition to the meaning of leadership and governance in our Bar Association.

MAC:dar

Cordially.

Живет

MICHEL A. COCCIA

APPELLATE COURT OF ILLINOIS
RICHARD J. DALEY CENTER
60602

CHAMBERS OF
JUSTICE MICHEL A. COCCIA

312/793-5403

May 22, 1989

Mr. Warren G. Lupel
Lupel & Bunn
30 North La Salle Street, #2000
Chicago, IL 60602

Dear Warren:

Congratulations to you for your outstanding effort and success in running for
the Assembly of the Illinois State Bar
Association.

I am simply thrilled with the fact that
you are interested in the management of our
Illinois State Bar Association.

I look forward to watching your illus-
trious career with the Bar and only hope that
you will continue on with the giving of more
definition to the meaning of leadership and
governance in our Bar Association.

Cordially,

MICHEL A. COCCIA

MAC:dsr

Leonard F. Amari

218 NORTH JEFFERSON, CHICAGO, ILLINOIS 60661, (312) 90650

September 30, 1991

Mr. Warren Lupel

Kats, Randall & Weinberg 200 N. LaSalle St., Ste. 2300 Chicago, Illinois 60601

Dear Warren:

The other evening, as I usually do, I began reading my non-essential mail at home after dinner while watching television. One of the items to be read was the most recent issue of the Illinois Bar Journal. Lo and behold, I came across the first article in the journal written by you with your ugly mug prominently displayed. Certainly, the article was very informative and helpful to the practicing bar. We are fortunate to have a man of your caliber contributing to our ISBA publications and for being so involved in our legal community.

However, and on a personal note, I cannot begin to tell you the pride that I felt (and continually feel) in knowing that the two of us have become so prominent in this legal community. We both began from such humble beginnings and have distinguished ourselves and are greatly respected in our profession. started together at Jack Marshall in 1965 and did the Knowing that we bulk of the trip together makes me especially proud and pleased.

You have always served as a great strength and role model for me and I take such great pride in the impact we have made in our profession. But for you, I could possibly have ended up as did David Shields. inspiration to You have been an me and, early on, demonstrated Importance of integrity, quality and generosity. be forever in your debt and always your greatest fan. relish our relationship, its duration and its depth.

Very truly yours,

Leonard F. Amari LFA/pkc

Leonard F. Amari

218 NORTH JEFFERSON, CHICAGO, ILLINOIS 60661, (312) 906-8560

September 30, 1991

Mr. Warren Lupel
Katz, Randall & Weinberg
200 N. LaSalle St., Ste. 2300
Chicago, Illinois 60601

Dear Warren:

The other evening, as I usually do, I began reading my non-essential mail at home after dinner while watching television. One of the items to be read was the most recent issue of the Illinois Bar Journal. Lo and behold, I came across the first article in the journal written by you with your ugly mug prominently displayed. Certainly, the article was very informative and helpful to the practicing bar. We are fortunate to have a man of your caliber contributing to our ISBA publications and for being so involved in our legal community.

However, and on a personal note, I cannot begin to tell you the pride that I felt (and continually feel) in knowing that the two of us have become so prominent in this legal community. We both began from such humble beginnings and have distinguished ourselves and are greatly respected in our profession. Knowing that we started together at Jack Marshall in 1965 and did the bulk of the trip together makes me especially proud and pleased.

You have always served as a great strength and role model for me and I take such great pride in the impact we have made in our profession. But for you, I could possibly have ended up as did David Shields. You have been an inspiration to me and, early on, demonstrated the importance of integrity, quality and generosity. I will be forever in your debt and always your greatest fan. I relish our relationship, its duration and its depth.

Very truly yours,

Leonard F. Amari

LFA/pkc

166

Franco A. Coladipietro

ONE TIFFANY PONTE

SUITE 912 1630307-370R 6/27/03

Warren- Thanks for the nice mate regarding My partnership. This letter overdue new about but 15 long I just received my persone Stationary

All the nice things Leonard says you don't do your justice - you've always been a wonderful friend/ Mentor to Me and I appreciate it Ciao - Franco

Franco A. Coladipietro
ONE TIFFANY POINTE
SUITE G12
BLOOMINGDALE, ILLINOIS 60108
(630) 307-3702
FAC@AMARI-LOCALLD.COM

6/27/03

Warren -

Thanks for the nice note regarding my partnership. This letter is long overdue but I just received my new personal stationary

All the nice things Leonard says about you don't do you justice - you've always been a wonderful friend/ mentor to me and I appreciate it.

Ciao -

Franco

CHARLES E. PORCELLINO

CIRCUIT COURT OF COOK COUNTY

6.17.98

ROLLING MEADOWLING

Dear Women:

"The measure of a mans Life in how he spends it."

Always The properacional, always The gentleman

The Humanitarian

You.

Always

It is an honor to know

Dellet read "Life in

ساء

God Blessing to

You and There you touched. Charlie

CIRCUIT COURT OF COOK COUNTY

CHARLES E. PORCELLINO
ASSOCIATE JUDGE

6·17·98

2121 EUCLID AVENUE
ROLLING MEADOWS, ILLINOIS 60008

Dear Warren:

"The measure of a mans
Life is how he spends it."

Always The professional,
always The gentleman - Always
The Humanitarian

It is an honor to know
you.
    I just read "Life in
a Delhi Slum" —

God's Blessings to
You and Those you touched.

Charlie

Leonard F. Amari

734 North Wells Street, Chicago, Illinois 60610. (312) 255-8550

February 26, 2001

Warren Lupel, Esq. 333 W. Wacker Dr. Suite 1800

Chicago, IL 60606

Dear Warren:

Thank you very much for your call, relative to the Italian Cultural Center "Man of the Year" honor. There aren't 5 people during my entire life who have had as positive an impact on me as you have. From you I learned integrity, intellectual honesty, and more important than anything else, decency. Warren, the mutual respect and sincere affection we have for one another is extraordinarily gratifying. Thanks for your nice call.

All the best,

Leonard F. Amari

734 North Wells Street. Chicago, Illinois 60610. (312) 255-8550

February 26, 2001

Warren Lupel, Esq.
333 W. Wacker Dr.
Suite 1800
Chicago, IL. 60606

Dear Warren:

Thank you very much for your call, relative to the Italian Cultural Center "Man of the Year" honor. There aren't 5 people during my entire life who have had as positive an impact on me as you have. From you I learned integrity, intellectual honesty, and more important than anything else, decency. Warren, the mutual respect and sincere affection we have for one another is extraordinarily gratifying. Thanks for your nice call.

All the best,

State of Illinois Circuit Court of Cook County

Robert E. Gordon Judge

1403 Richard J. Daley Center

Chicago, Illinois 60602

(312) 603-4157

WARREN:

SomeTimes" "Thank you" you will be a is DT fait for enough but Life, and Some lay to repay your kinds. I wish you and you fruity histsty or happy Yes.

State of Illinois
Circuit Court of Cook County

Robert E. Gordon
Judge

1403 Richard J. Daley Center
Chicago, Illinois 60602
(312) 603-4157

WARREN

Sometimes "Thank you" is not enough but you will be a friend for life, and someday I hope to repay your kindness. I wish you and your family a healthy and happy new year.

Regards,

Bob

BRET RAPPAPORT SUITE #700

180 NORTH LA SALLE STREET CHICAGO, ILLINOIS 60601

November 12, 2003

Warren Lupel

Kate Randall Weinberg & Richmond 333 West Wacker Drive, Suite 1800 Chicago, IL 60606

Dear Warren:

I love what I do. Being a lawyer, helping people, solving problems, arguing legal issues, research, and all the rest is what I do and enjoy. Unfortunately, a lot of times, opponents dispense with courtesy and professionalism. They do so because they think it serves their clients or makes them feel more powerful; or maybe their mothers and fathers didn't teach them manners or the Golden Rule.

That's a long rambling introduction to a simple "thank you". Thank you for your professionalism, courtesy and dogged determination to litigate this case on the issues and the law. My father was the kind of lawyer you are and far from compromising tactics or strategy, such an ethic serves the client by focusing the case on the law and facts. There are far too few like you left.

It has been a pleasure to cross-swords with you. I look forward to crossing paths again.

Take care.

BAR/We

213828999100-0

Bret A. Rappaport

BRET RAPPAPORT
SUITE 2700
180 NORTH LA SALLE STREET
CHICAGO, ILLINOIS 60601

November 12, 2003

Warren Lupel
Katz Randall Weinberg & Richmond
333 West Wacker Drive, Suite 1800
Chicago, IL 60606

Dear Warren:

I love what I do. Being a lawyer, helping people, solving problems, arguing legal issues, research, and all the rest is what I do and enjoy. Unfortunately, a lot of times, opponents dispense with courtesy and professionalism. They do so because they think it serves their clients or makes them feel more powerful; or maybe their mothers and fathers didn't teach them manners or the Golden Rule.

That's a long rambling introduction to a simple "thank you". Thank you for your professionalism, courtesy and dogged determination to litigate this case on the issues and the law. My father was the kind of lawyer you are and far from compromising tactics or strategy, such an ethic serves the client by focusing the case on the law and facts. There are far too few like you left.

It has been a pleasure to cross-swords with you. I look forward to crossing paths again.

Take care,

Bret A. Rappaport

BAR/wc

215828.1 999102-00895

176

12/20/80

Dear Warren,

This is a letter of congratulatringe and Law Jackly since the g very your filt the Year Award""" It to one that this was Velasked there were Test Lawyer my mind that a douft are truly, the not you know lawye Right detals experience as a homar all kinds albugs, a na Christma all thank d to thank youth for understanding, for you Flam sure your Sie reward for and och Love, and wonderful Perpect My family and of love you) Aggie

2/20/80

Dear Warren,

This is a letter of congratulations on your "Lawyer of the Year Award." It was very shocking to me that this was your first award, since the awards were started. There has never been a doubt in my mind that you are truly the best Lawyer, every year, not only in your office but right along LaSalle St. I know lawyers, and I think I speak from experience as a woman that deals with all kinds of attorneys.

Thank you for a nice Christmas Party, and for including me in your party. Thank you for your friendship, and most of all Thank you for your understanding, for you really understand me.

May God Bless you always for your kindness and your Goodness. I am sure he has his reward for you and your wonderful family.

With Love and Respect,

(My family and I love you very much!)

Aggie

178

Shawn S. Kasserman

33 North Dearborn Street

Chicago, Illinois 00002
12-10-10

Warren I loved that you recieval the Honorary Fellows Award. I loved your comments and the emotion behind them. I love that You are such a wonderful example, for our profession. And mest love that you are a friend & Mine. Your concern for those in need is You up are a with So genuine, that you follow it your actions is heroic. vole model for me, my promise to you is that the dedication you have will Always continue on You have домен through the example us all to follow. Your FRUND, Shuner

Shawn S. Kasserman
33 North Dearborn Street
Chicago, Illinois 60602

12-10-10

Warren —

I loved that you received the Honorary
Fellows Award. I loved your comments and
the emotion behind them. I love that
you are such a wonderful example for
our profession. And most of all I
love that you are a friend of mine!

Your concern for those i need is
so genuine, that you follow it up with
your actions is heroic. You are a
role model for me, my promise to you
is that the dedication you have will
always continue on through the example
you have given us all to follow

Your Fellow,
Shawn

180

STATE OF ILLINOIS

CLERK OF THE SUPREME COURT SPRINGFIELD

December 15, 2010

Dear Warren,

The flown are beautiful! The bright yellow rous and subtle are the perfect antidote to this gloomy December weather. Thank you for brightening my day with gesture and your very green and white hydrangear a your thoughtful message. working with you through the you how, indeed been a pleasure. your unfiibing Courtery and profeccionatum. how been appreciated by my staff and me. Thank you. Best wisher, always.

P.S. Lam no read that our paths crossreal at the ARC on Friday.

December 15, 2010

Dear Warren,

The flowers are beautiful! The bright yellow roses and subtle green and white hydrangeas are the perfect antidote to this gloomy December weather. Thank you for brightening my day with your kind gesture and your very thoughtful message.

Working with you through the years has, indeed, been a pleasure. Your unfailing courtesy and professionalism has been appreciated by my staff and me. Thank you.

Best wishes, always

Juleann

P.S. I am so pleased that our paths crossed at the ARDC on Friday.

Forrest S. Bayard

150 NORTHWACKER DRIVE SUITE 270 CHICAGO,

November 4, 1998

Warren Lupel

79 W. Monroe Street, Suite 903

Chicago, IL 60603

Dear Sonny

Thanks for thinking of me and providing the opportunity to be a fellow for the Illinois Bar Foundation. Count me in. Enclosed is my check for $100 which will be forthcoming every year until my $1000 pledge is complete. Sonny, you are an outstanding lawyer and an awesome human being. Thanks for supporting me in my work, providing me with ongoing advice and most of all for being my friend. It is a privileged to support you and the Illinois Bar Foundation.

Warm regards,

Forrest S. Bayard FSD0

Forrest S. Bayard

150 NORTH WACKER DRIVE • SUITE 2570 • CHICAGO, ILLINOIS 60606

November 4, 1998

Warren Lupel
79 W. Monroe Street, Suite 903
Chicago, IL 60603

Dear Sonny:

Thanks for thinking of me and providing the opportunity to be a fellow for the Illinois Bar Foundation. Count me in. Enclosed is my check for $100 which will be forthcoming every year until my $1000 pledge is complete.

Sonny, you are an outstanding lawyer and an awesome human being. Thanks for supporting me in my work, providing me with ongoing advice and most of all for being my friend. It is a priviledge to support you and the Illinois Bar Foundation.

Warm regards,

Forrest S. Bayard

FSB/bh:lupel.001
enc.

184

www.ingramcontent.com/pod-product-compliance
Lightning Source LLC
Chambersburg PA
CBHW051622120626
46551CB00014B/1906